TRASH
Cinema

A Celebration of
Overlooked Masterpieces

Edited by
Andrew J. Rausch
and **R.D. Riley**

Trash Cinema: A Celebration of Overlooked Masterpieces

Library of Congress Control Number: 2015908762

Published in the USA by:

BearManor Media
P.O. Box 71426
Albany, Georgia 31708
www.BearManorMedia.com

ISBN-10: 1-59393-821-7 (alk. paper)
ISBN-13: 978-1-59393-821-5 (alk. paper)

Design and Layout: Valerie Thompson

Table of Contents

Asylum (1972)
by E.D. Tucker

Amicus Productions always had the rather dubious, and debatably inaccurate, distinction of being a poor man's Hammer Films. While Amicus shared many talents in common with their higher profile competitor, they were wise enough to carve out a niche for themselves in the horror movie genre. One area in which they excelled was the anthology film where several short vignettes were tied together into a feature by some manner of framing story device. By the time they made *Asylum* in 1972, Amicus was probably the leading production company in the world for this type of format with films like *Dr. Terror's House of Horrors* (1965), *Torture Garden* (1967), and *House That Dripped Blood* (1970) already under their cinematic belts and their magnum opus, *Tales from the Crypt*, poised to be released that same year.

Asylum stands as one of Amicus's best anthology pictures due to the selection of short stories that make up its vignettes and the wonderful framing sequence, one of the best ever utilized for this type of film, which ties them all together. The stories came from the mind of *Psycho* scribe Robert Bloch and even though some of them were over thirty years old he was able to freshen them up nicely in his screenplay. Having the same person who wrote the individual tales do the framing device keeps everything uniform, but Bloch also managed to make it interesting while tying it in to one of the vignettes.

Asylum opens with young Dr. Martin arriving for a job interview at the remote asylum for the incurably insane run by Dr. Star. Expecting to meet with the proprietor, Martin is told by his assistant Dr. Rutherford that Star has himself gone insane and is now one of the asylum's patients. Rutherford informs Martin that Dr. Star has adapted an entirely new personality and if he can determine which patient is him from reviewing the cases of the four at the facility, he will be considered for the position. Accepting this challenge, Dr. Rutherford is introduced to the floor orderly, Max Reynolds, and locked into the ward with the patients to hear each of their stories.

The first tale, "Frozen Fear," is easily the most satisfying to horror fans and was heavily played up in the advertising materials. A man murders his wealthy wife and temporarily hides her dismembered body in the basement freezer wrapped in brown paper like meat from the butcher shop. Unfortunately he had not counted on her voodoo studies bringing her various pieces back to life and he and his mistress run afoul of the pissed off parts. This segment is surprisingly dry in the blood department but it is filmed so well that it really doesn't matter. The scene shifts seamlessly from the bludgeoned wife's hand in a death grip on the side of the freezer to her final part being wrapped and the blood mopped from the floor. The dismembered limbs writhing on the floor and severed head sucking air through the paper that surrounds it still hold up well today.

"The Weird Tailor" is the second segment and leans more towards fantasy than outright horror. It's not really the debt-ridden tailor who is weird here, but rather his customer, who requests a very precisely made suit of a strange luminous material. As it turns out, the buyer is an occultist who is trying to use the suit to revive the corpse of his deceased son that he just happens to have in his living room. An altercation between the tailor and his customer causes the man to join his son in death and the tailor to be stuck with a suit which brings the store mannequin to life after his wife decides to display it.

Batting third is "Lucy Comes to Stay," which is the most pedestrian and forgettable of the bunch. A woman recently released from another mental institution returns home to her brother's care and quickly becomes bored with her closely monitored existence. When her friend Lucy shows up and offers to help her escape from her dull predicament, most of the audience that is still awake will have guessed the surprise ending long before it arrives.

The final story, "Mannequins of Horror," is not told in flashbacks like the others but is instead integrated into the framing story. Dr.

Martin is introduced to Dr. Byron who is at the asylum for reasons that are never explained. As part of his therapy he is allowed to create small dolls with very detailed faces into which he is trying to transfer his soul to bring them to life. He demonstrates a hatred of Rutherford and that may be the reason he is bound to a wheelchair after an attack by an unidentified patient.

After meeting with this final inmate, Martin returns to Rutherford's office but rather than deliver a verdict he chastises the senior psychiatrist for not at least attempting to help his patients. Just as Rutherford is contemplating removing Byron's "dolls" and discontinuing what little therapy he has, one of the creepy creations stabs him in the back of the neck with scalpel and creates another vacancy at the asylum. When Martin stomps on the tiny terror he realizes that its insides are not the anticipated mechanical parts but rather miniature organs!

Curious to see if Byron did actually succeed in transferring his soul into his creation, Martin runs back to the ward to find him dead from being mysteriously crushed. He also finds out his conclusion as to Dr. Starr's identity really was a little too obvious and the mistake costs him his life. The final scene as the camera pulls back from the dreary estate that harbors the insane amid maniacal cackling gives a fitting end to the grim proceedings.

In addition to the solid stories, *Asylum* also boasts an excellent cast including such venerable British actors as Peter Cushing, Herbert Lom (he was Austrian but lived most of his life in England), and Patrick Magee. The rest of the cast includes Robert Powell as Dr. Martin, a pre-*Space: 1999* Barry Morse, Charlotte Rampling, and Britt Ekland. Also worth noting is actor Geoffrey Bayldon who plays the orderly. In addition to having turned down the title role in *Doctor Who* twice, he had just finished up a successful run in British children's series *Catweazle*. It must have been a shock for English kiddies to see him here in this dark horror film.

Asylum fared well at the box office during its initial release but it was overshadowed by Amicus's most successful anthology picture, the EC Comics based *Tales from the Crypt*, which was released the same year. In 1979, Dynamite Entertainment—a distribution company which had been enjoying some success scavenging later Hammer films that had seen little or no exposure stateside, re-released *Asylum* under the far more lurid title *House of Crazies*. The revamped advertising campaign not only went to great lengths to spell out everything audiences would be in for but also spoiled the film's twist ending to anyone paying close attention.

Based on the success of *Asylum* and *Tales from the Crypt*, Amicus would continue to turn out anthology pictures for the next few years before switching over to a cycle of films based on Edgar Rice Burroughs's novels including *The Land that Time Forgot* and *At the Earth's Core*. Their final film was 1980's *Monster Club* which tried to return to the anthology mode with only mediocre results.

The Baby (1973)
by Brad Paulson

A social worker pushes for an assignment that brings her closer to an adult baby. Can you blame her?

This film is an unadulterated classic. It was made back in the day when low budget movies were actually shot on film. In 1973, the man who brought us *Beneath the Planet of the Apes, Magnum Force,* and four episodes of to-date the best TV series ever, *The Twilight Zone,* bestowed upon us the wonderful gift to cinema that is *The Baby.* His name was Ted Post and I don't know if this movie was the result of his or the writer's (Abe Polsky) drug binge (there was a lot of acid going around in those days), or what exactly inspired it, but God bless its muse. There's nothing else like this film out there.

This was a very obscure film before Netflix added it to their streaming catalog. I remember going to Suncoast Video years ago after we had finished *The Bloodstained Bride* and being told it was available in stores. I went to our local mall twice a week for a month and never saw it. What I did see on the shelf in the B-section for horror was a multi-pack of films that *The Baby* was part of. The image on the cover made an imprint on my mind: an ominous looking crib with man sized legs hanging out of it accompanied by an arm holding a bloody axe.

"Wait," I told myself. "Is this a movie about an adult baby?" "No," I quickly responded to my own question. "It's a movie about a killer adult baby!" "Oh, this could be good," the inner dialogue intensified. My fascination with *The Baby* kept growing as I teetered on the edge of buying it, but declined time after time, convinced that it would either be shitty or boring. Little did I know, I was keeping myself from an absolute, under-the-radar gem.

The day finally arrived that *The Bloodstained Bride* made it to my local Suncoast. I remember being thrilled to see it, but then looking over and seeing *The Baby* vying for my attention. If I would have just bought it right then and there, my curiosity would have been satisfied. But I didn't. However, the image on that box cover was stuck in my mind and it stayed there as the years passed. Before long it had woven its way into my psyche as I found my fascination with not only the movie, but adult babies in general growing. I never stopped thinking about that movie. I was like Ryan Gosling in *The Notebook* (except for the fact I look nothing like him), dwelling on a lost love I couldn't have.

And then one glorious day I saw that Netflix added *The Baby* to streaming. I immediately watched it and was instantly pissed off at myself for keeping myself from this treasure all those years. Nine times out of ten I would have been right about predicting a movie like this to be shittiness, but not in this case. In this case, I was wrong for ever doubting it. But then again that's what makes movies like these so interesting. When you're garbage diving you're going to get pretty filthy. Occasionally, however, you're going to find some gold.

After watching, I also realized this movie is an anomaly because it functions as both a drive-in movie and an effective drama. How many times can you say this about underground cinema marketed as low-budget exploitation horror?

As *The Baby* opens with social worker Ann Gentry looking at pictures of a young child over a sweeping rich score, there's a gothic feel to the piece. It's like one of those Roger Corman movies he adapted from the Poe classics. The pictures span over time until the baby becomes an adult, looking through the bars of his crib, appearing confused, trapped and wounded.

Gentry is played with wonderfully convincing empathy by Anjanette Comer. From the first scene she is fascinated with the case before she's even officially on it. When she arrives at the house of the baby, she meets two really hot sisters, Germaine (Marianna Hill) and Alba (Suzanne Zenor) Wadsworth, and their mother, Mrs. Wadsworth (the Joan-Crawford-esque Ruth Roman). We get the sense that weird shit's going on, despite Mrs. Wadsworth playing it cool and relaxed as she welcomes Ann into her home.

Gentry doesn't waste much time before she starts asking questions about the family's relationship with the adult baby.

"I notice you call him Baby and the case history doesn't show any other name. What is his real name?" asks Ann.

"Just Baby," replies Mrs. Wadsworth.

Referring to a grown man as Baby sets off a few red flags, and even more when Ann finds out the only real income the family has is what the county gives them for Baby, which is hilarious because the three adults in the house are essentially sponging off of the baby.

We find out that Mrs. Wadsworth is a little bitter because her husband took off and left the family right before Baby was born. More red flags. And yet more when Ann asks to see Baby and spots nervous glances between Mrs. Wadsworth and Germaine. Mrs. Wadsworth soon takes Ann upstairs where her son (a fully-grown man) sleeps in a crib while dressed like a baby.

Ann lays wide eyes upon the bizarre scenario and instantly has a case of the adult baby bug. From that moment forward, she's a regular visitor at the Wadsworth home. Doing so adds an element of unease to how the family reacts to her. Especially since the workers prior to Gentry would only visit the house twice a year. Now Ann's showing up like she's kin. She volunteers to spoon feed the baby under the psychotic, leering eyes of sister Germaine. Is it jealousy in her eyes or just simple bat-shit craziness?

Even stranger is when Gentry witnesses Mrs. Wadsworth massaging the baby's legs so his muscles won't go bad even though that big bugaboo has been crawling like he's been training for a marathon.

The red flags keep raising as Ann's boss becomes concerned when he sees she's spending so much time with Baby. He recommends she ease back a bit and concentrate more on her emergency cases. To make matters worse, we learn that the last social worker who looked too much into the Baby case vanished and was never found again. This strangely doesn't seem to bother her boss at all, nor Ann for that matter. She's got the full-fledged adult baby bug. We can see it in her eyes. Once you go adult baby, you can never be bothered with regular social worker cases again!

By this point in the movie it's becoming challenging to keep track of how many red flags have been raised. All of which Ann is too busy to recognize because she's been busy going back and forth from the Wadsworth house playing with Baby. She segues this play time into covertly trying to see if Baby can walk by playing fetch with the ball. This does not go unnoticed by the sisters as Alba drags Baby away while he protests. And can you blame him? His evil sister took his teddy bear away, the heartless wretch!

Unfortunately, Baby's positive role model Ann has some problems of her own, which probably has to do with why she's so personally interested in the case. These issues are dug up a bit as Germaine walks her out and lays psycho eyes on her as she asks about her husband. Ann switches the conversation to Baby and Germaine invites her to go hiking. I'm unsure whether the invite is lesbian date night related or if Germaine just wants to take Ann up in the woods and push her off the cliff. Regardless, Ann declines, which is clearly the smartest decision she's made in the entire movie up to this point. (Unless, of course, Germaine's invitation really was all about lesbian date night.)

As Ann drives away from the Wadsworth house, we see how derailed she really is as she thinks of her husband. Then Baby. Then the husband. Then back to Baby as she's driving home. She arrives home and settles in to drink and watch slides of her husband as her mother-in-law sits there quietly in the background.

Ann is clearly riddled with guilt by something that happened to her husband. She sobs relentlessly as she's comforted by her mother in law. Perhaps this is another connection for her to Baby? She lives with her mother-in-law and Baby lives with his mother. Both are grown-ups living in respective states of infancy.

Enter an attractive Vicki Lawrence-esque babysitter hired to watch Baby as the Wadsworth ladies go out on the town. The adult baby babysitter sloths about watching TV while Baby is upstairs in his crib. She's on the phone with her boyfriend, who's trying to get laid and pushing it every step of the way.

"No, Billy you can't come over. You know about the freak."

But that darned Billy just won't listen. He keeps going for broke as the sitter replies, "Now what kind of a question is that? You know I'm wearing panties." More of what I could only assume to be relentless begging for sex from Billy ensues as the adult baby babysitter agrees to drop by his place when she's done and gets him off the phone by saying, "Listen, I have to go see about the baby."

The adult baby's babysitter follows the sound of his crying into the nursery and discovers he has a wet diaper. She changes it for him and powders him to boot. This is what I would call an all-purpose babysitter! As Baby pounds on his crib distressed, she lets him out and he immediately books it right for the door. By the way, this would be red flag I-don't-even-know-how-many by now that there is something very wrong happening in this house. She tries to bring him back to the crib and the clumsy adult baby bonks his head.

He bawls relentlessly and she picks him up and attempts to comfort him by kissing him on his forehead. This act either cranks his adult baby engine into gear or he figures since he's stuck there he may as well try and score. Baby immediately attempts vitamin D withdrawal. At first the adult baby babysitter protests, but then seems not to mind. I'm unsure whether this is fetish related or because it's the most effective way she knows to stop the crying.

Mrs. Wadsworth and her daughters return home just in time to catch Baby and the sitter in the middle of naughty play time. Their reaction reveals just how twisted their relationship is with Baby. Not only does Baby get diaper-blocked but Mrs. Wadsworth goes full Crawford on the sitter. Instead of trying to stop her actions, the sisters defend her.

"You tell anybody about this and we'll press charges!" warn the sisters to the adult baby babysitter. "You were abusing a mental case and that's a criminal offense!" And the best bullshit excuse award for beating the crap out of a babysitter and spinning it to somehow be her fault goes to…the Wadsworth family!

Meanwhile Ann continues to seek help for Baby. She attempts to get the hot blonde sister on her side with unsuccessful results. The reply she gets is, "Baby was born backwards. He's been that way all his life. And that's all there is to it."

The tensions between Ann and Mrs. Wadsworth continue to escalate as Ann suspects Baby is being kept from any emotional development whatsoever. Baby is not treated well by sister Alba. She uses what looks like a cattle prod against him for cooperating with Ann.

Germaine on the other hand, seems to have more of a soft spot for Baby and proves this by removing her clothing and crawling into the crib with him when it's time to go nite-nite. However, the act isn't technically considered incest since Ann is a sister from another father. In fact, we learn that all three siblings are from different fathers. For some strange reason, each guy must have found Mrs. Wadsworth a tad controlling.

Ann tries a new strategy to help Baby by setting up a meeting with the Wadsworth family and her supervisors. Not only are they a no show, they file a complaint against her. In a bout of bravery, Ann goes back to the house of the baby, tells Mrs. Wadsworth what she thinks of her and that she's going to sic the public guardian on her. She also mentions that she intends fighting her for the custody of Baby.

Ann does not leave that house on good terms with Mrs. Wadsworth, but her threat about the guardian seems to work as Mrs. Wadsworth calls for a peace treaty and invites her to a birthday party they're having for Baby.

Ann makes the poor decision of attending and finds herself surrounded by a bunch of swinger-looking types as flute style porn music plays in the background. Baby looks very confused as everyone has a good time and brings him a cake.

As the party kicks into gear, bad 70s dancing occurs as the Wadsworth family attempts to push alcohol on Ann. She refuses, wanting to have her full faculties, but her request to talk about Baby is delayed by Mrs. Wadsworth as she gives her the brush off and hits on several different guys at the same time. Ann herself gets harassed by a sleazy guy with terrible, yet amusing pickup lines. "Lady, there's only one thing I see in those big, beautiful, cat eyes: hunger."

"Buzz off creep. There's a difference between hunger and starvation." Ann retorts.

It doesn't take long before the sisters are able to switch Ann's drink and drag her off into another room. Ann wakes tied up. Baby wanders into the room and finds her. He removes Ann's mouth gag but finds himself too preoccupied with his own drooling and idiotic babbling to untie her.

Back at the party, hot Alba is having quite the time with a sleazy guy. They innocently flirt with one another.

"Will you do it the way I like it?" Alba asks.

"Does a cannibal eat raw meat?" the sleazy guy responds.

"Okay, cannibal. Let's test your appetite."

Things seem to be going well for the sleazy guy until crazy-ass Alba wants to put a lighter flame under his finger.

"I'll do anything to get to paradise, but does it have to be in an ambulance?" the sleazy guy asks.

Apparently it does because Alba seems to get off on this sort of thing.

Despite the sleazy guy's cheesy lines (although, people did legitimately talk like that back then), the rest of the movie is played very straightforward and that's one of the many things I love about it. Especially the fact that they take this approach and it works.

While Alba is involved in psychotic finger burning foreplay with the sleazy guy, Ann locates a hacksaw and uses it on her ropes. Some help the baby was on that. It made me want to yell at the screen "Thanks, Baby, you useless asshole!" However, despite Baby's lack of assistance, Ann does manage to escape and take him with her even though the idiot is half drooling in a corner of the room playing with his teddy bear. Note to villains: if you have to leave the hero in a room alone, remove all weapons and/or implements of escape.

Ann and Baby make it out of the house before Mama and the sisters kick everyone out of the party, the most difficult of course being the sleazy guy. To their great dismay, they discover Ann driving off with Baby in the car. Mrs. Wadsworth and her daughters are about to chase her, but discover their tires have been slashed. Mama seems to have an odd kind of respect for Ann as she utters, "She thinks of everything" and "I'm beginning to understand that girl" after the sisters are puzzled trying to figure out why she wouldn't just go to the police. At this point Mrs. Wadsworth and Ann are basically on opposite sides of the same coin, each vying for possession of Baby.

Ann takes Baby home, gives him a bath and puts him in a suit. She does not go to the cops. Mrs. Wadsworth is devastated by the loss of her adult baby. Hot blonde daughter Alba doesn't help matters much when she mentions to Mama that they should have let the circus sideshow take Baby when they had the chance.

Grinding the salt even deeper into her wounds, Mrs. Wadsworth receives a letter from Ann that reads: "In a short time the Baby you once knew will no longer exist." Ann doesn't stop there. She drives her "fuck you" message home to Mrs. Wadsworth loud and clear by closing the letter with "Your baby is lost to you forever."

Mrs. Wadsworth falls into Ann's trap, takes her daughters and heads for Ann's house to attack her in the dark of night. The sisters enter the house while Mrs. Wadsworth stays in the car.

As Germaine moves through the house there's an air of creepiness as she follows the sounds of a crying baby. To me, this is the greatest wandering through a house while weird sounds occur in the background scene ever. Mama finally gets freaked and decides to enter the house herself. She finds her daughters dead and gets herself in a fight with the not only prepared Ann, but also her mother-in-law. Axe and fire poker fight ensues with an added cleaver assist from mother-in-law. Wanting to take Mrs. Wadsworth alive as she claims she has broken legs, Ann has her killer lackey back off.

Ann and her mother-in-law ruthlessly bury Mrs. Wadsworth alive next to her dead daughters. This made me remember that during this time films with incredibly disturbing subject matter and tone were rated PG.

With the threat to Baby now eliminated, Ann is free to keep him as her own. Yet, we discover that what we thought to be a compassionate social worker, a woman who has fought so hard to remove Baby from his imprisonment, has harbored selfish intentions. She brings Baby into a room she has converted into a nursery and introduces him to her husband—a man who suffered such devastating injuries from the car accident that Ann was responsible for, he has become an adult baby. To Ann this is the perfect happy ending. She has a playmate for her husband and from the way she hugs and kisses both men on the lips, perhaps even something else.

This is one of the most unique surprise endings ever captured on film. Especially from a mainstream director like Post.

The Baby is a film of brilliance that's way ahead of its time. It elevates the drive-in genre it's advertised among. It's an under-the-radar exploitation movie that takes a serious approach and pulls it off magnificently. It utilizes subtlety and great performances. David Manzy does an utterly outstanding job playing the lead role of Baby. His performance is 99% dialogue free and it is perfect. If an adult baby acting school ever opens, he should be their poster child—the Marlon Brando of adult baby actors.

The only thing I don't like about *The Baby* is the fact the distributors marketed it as a killer adult baby movie and, although that would make a great movie, it's not this one. The box cover is misleading. The adult baby was innocent. It was all the people supposedly trying to help him that were the real villains.

Get yourself a date and treat them to a screening of *The Baby*. If they stay for the entire film, they may just be the one for you (either that or you'll need a restraining order). And, if you bring a pair of diapers, neither one of you will even have to get up to go to the bathroom!

The Black Six (1974)
by David Walker

On paper, it must've seemed like a great idea—take two popular film genres (blaxploitation and outlaw biker), mash 'em together, and then throw in a cast of six NFL players, all ready to kick whitey's ass. There's no way this combination of elements, seemingly blessed by the gods of exploitation cinema, could not have seemed like a sure hit. And to be clear, the definition of "sure hit" must be contextualized within the framework of an era in American film when low budget, independently produced features often were financed from questionable revenue sources looking to launder money from ill-gotten gains. This is not to say that *The Black Six* was financed with money from tax-shelter-seeking investors or Mafia dons looking to wash their dirty money, because that's not the case. No, *The Black Six* is merely one of the most potentially brilliant blaxploitation films of all time, produced under a series of quality-limiting factors, which sadly resulted in the film's inability to become the work of genius it could have been.

The Black Six starts with the violent murder of high school student Eddie Daniels (Robert Howard) by a gang of redneck bikers who aren't too happy that a young black man is consorting with a white girl. Word of Eddie's death reaches his older brother Bubba (Gene Washington), a disillusioned veteran of the war in Vietnam, who has not been home in years. Bubba has taken to a nomadic life of tooling around the country with five of his fellow vets, who round out this war-weary motorcycle gang. Bubba and his crew have seen enough violence in 'Nam, and they would love to leave the killing behind them. Despite the threat of the racist bikers who killed Eddie, however, Bubba and his friends—Junior Bro Williams (Carl

Eller), Frenchy LaBoise (Lem Barney), Bookie Garrett (Mercury Morris), Tommy Bunka (Willie Lanier), and Kevin Washington ("Mean" Joe Greene)—decide something must be done. The murder of Eddie demands either justice or revenge—or both—and the Black Six are just the guys to dispense fistfuls of each.

The brainchild of writer-producer-director Matt Cimber, *The Black Six* is a shining example of everything that is both right and wrong with the blaxploitation films of the 1970s. It is an earnest attempt at making an exploitation movie which seems to have something to say—though it's not clear exactly what that something is. With Cimber's story, inspired by Alfred Lord Tennyson's poem "The Charge of the Light Brigade," and a screenplay by Mikel Angel (a.k.a. George Theakos), *The Black Six* holds the promise of weighing in on some heavy subjects. First, there's the murder of Eddie. To be clear, the killing of Eddie is a modern-day lynching. He is murdered because he did not "know" his place, recalling the real life slayings of countless other African-Americans, whose crimes were often nothing more than looking at a white woman. Then there is the commentary on returning war vets incapable of fitting back in with mainstream American society. And finally, there is the message of justice for the black man in America. All of this is hinted at, but never fully explored, making it unclear if *The Black Six* is actually trying to say something. If there is in fact a message, it is largely lost under the crushing weight of a poorly written script, a cast of non-actors, and half-assed production values, all brought together on a shoe-string budget. But as any true fan of exploitation films can tell you, the shortcomings and ineptitudes that don't kill certain movies only makes them better. Such is the case of *The Black Six*.

With two of the biggest blaxploitation stars being Jim Brown and Fred Williamson—both ex-NFL players—it must have seemed like a stroke of pure genius to cast a film with six NFL players. Unfortunately, even the combined strength of Washington, Eller, Barney, Morris, Lanier, and Greene is barely enough to carry *The Black Six*. This is not meant to dismiss the acting of the main cast, because it isn't really their fault. Though Brown and Williamson were the biggest stars to come out of professional football, they weren't alone. Bernie Casey (*Hit Man*) was a professional ball player, as was Tony King (*Gordon's War*), and Carl Weathers, who would go on to stardom in

Rocky, after a string of supporting roles in movies like *Friday Foster* and *Bucktown*. There was also Tim Brown and Roy Jefferson, who starred in lesser-known blaxploitation entries *Black Heat* and *Brotherhood of Death*, respectively. It is clear that the biggest problem with *The Black Six* is not the limited acting chops of the cast, but the writing, direction, and overall production of the film.

With the deck stacked against *The Black Six*, it's a wonder the film works as well as it does. And to be perfectly honest, there are moments to be found in this film that could almost be confused with cinematic brilliance. In one standout scene, the black bikers try to order ham sandwiches and Pabst Blue Ribbon from a bar, only to be denied service by the racist owner. Left with little choice, the gang does what anyone would do in this situation—they literally tear the place down, while the owner screams, "Help, help, the niggers are tearin' down my bar!"

It's moments like this—crafted with all the quality and attention to acting and direction found in porn from the same era—that gives *The Black Six* its oddball charm. And if the film simply had more scenes like this one, it would be a priceless gem. That's not to say this is a good film, because it really isn't, although it is better than so many other genre entries. It could be argued that whatever redeeming qualities there are to be found in *The Black Six* comes from it the fact that when it comes to blaxploitation flicks the bar is set ridiculously low. For all of its shortcomings, *The Black Six* will never be as bad as *Speeding Up Time*, or *The Guy from Harlem*. Truth be told, however, it's not the comparison to the gutbucket quality of lesser Z-grade black action films that gives *The Black Six* whatever quirky charm it has. No, for lack of any other better description, this is a film that simply refuses to be as terrible as it should be. Other films, like *Blackenstein* and *Velvet Smooth*, give up the ghost without even trying—as if merely aspiring to be entertaining is too much work. Despite everything working against it, however, *The Black Six* never stops trying to entertain, even when it is terrible.

Blood of Dracula's Castle (1969)
by E.D. Tucker

By the late 1960s, the fledging film production company Independent International had already begun to make a name for itself in the exploitation film market. While partners Sam Sherman and Al Adamson only had one feature to their credit at this point, *Satan's Sadists* had come in on the cutting edge of the new violent biker movie trend that was currently sweeping the drive-in theater circuit. Hoping to cash in on the always popular horror genre, Adamson had procured a story treatment called *Feast of the Vampires* and writer Rex Carlton was brought in to translate the tale of cannibal vampires into a screenplay. The finished film may not have retained much of the original story, but it did prove to be one of director Adamson's most coherent productions and a popular item in theaters and on television for many years to come. Sadly, *Blood of Dracula's Castle* would also end up being a black eye for Independent International and a source of financial disappointment.

On a meager budget estimated to be around $60,000, Sherman and Adamson were able to secure both an excellent location and an impressive cast. Shea Castle (also known as Sky Castle) was built in the Southern California desert near Del Sur by a real estate tycoon in the early 1920s. The imposing structure was modeled after medieval Irish castles and came complete with a lake and its own private air strip. Tales of supernatural phenomenon still surround the site and at least one death by suicide has been confirmed within its walls. It was at this architectural curiosity that Adamson assembled his equally curious cast of veteran actors and members of his ever growing repertory company.

Alex D'Arcy (*Horrors of Spider Island*) and Paula Raymond (*Beast From 20,000 Fathoms*), both of whose long careers were nearly at an end, were cast as Count and Countess Townsend (a.k.a Dracula). Robert Dix (*Forbidden Planet*) played the psychopath Johnny who in some versions of the film even turns out to be a werewolf! At the last minute, veteran horror actor John Carradine was added for name value and (mis)cast as George the butler. While Carradine makes everything he can out of a throwaway role, it seems almost impossible that he could appear in this film at all and *not* play Dracula! The remaining cast, including Gene O'Shea, Barbara Bishop, and Vicki Volante all give performances in excess of the film's low budget. This combination of cast and location made it look like there was far more on the screen than the cost conscious Independent International had really spent.

Blood of Dracula's Castle is the tale of modern day vampires, who may be the original Count and Countess Dracula, living in an isolated desert castle. To survive, they capture young women, who are then chained in their dungeon basement and drained of their blood through the most modern of techniques. At some point in history, the Draculas apparently became mixed up with the cult of the moon goddess Luna. Whenever things get boring around the castle, they sacrifice one of their blood slaves with the help of their butler George, who just happens to be a high priest. Also on hand for laughs are Mango the mute hunchback and Johnny the recently escaped homicidal killer/werewolf. Things get complicated when a young couple inherit the castle and decide they want to evict the current tenants and live there themselves. By the end of the film the vampires, who seem a little too civilized for their own good, and their associates are dispatched and the young heroes are left to ponder if they really want to live in a castle out in the middle of the desert after all.

Director Al Adamson manages to infuse some unique and unconventional touches that give the film a charm all its own. The vampires only drink blood from wine glasses after their butler has extracted it from their victims with a large syringe. When they meet their end by turning to dust in the light of the sun, the Count and Countess turn into bats and fly off into the castle. The final moments of the film are a Mango-fest as the hulking brute is shot, hit with an axe, set on fire, *and* shoved off a cliff. Hopefully actor Ray Young got a bonus for that day's work!

Unfortunately, after the film was completed it became locked in legal turmoil. The financial backers had this film and another one, *Nightmare in Wax*, starring an eye-patched Cameron Mitchell as a demented artist, in production at the same time. When *Nightmare* ran into financial problems with the lab that the backers could not resolve, it was trapped in legal limbo. *Blood of Dracula's Castle* had been cross collateralized with *Nightmare* in the finance arrangement so it was stuck, too. A distributor called Crown International eventually paid off the lab costs and obtained the rights to both films, which they played on a very successful double bill. Independent International lost all rights to the picture and spent years competing against their own product for drive-in rentals.

After a long and successful theatrical run, the film was syndicated to television by two different companies in two different versions. One version, from Crown International, is the same as the one they distributed to theaters, and the character of Johnny is just an ordinary psychopath with a fixation on the moon. In the other version, credited to Paragon International Pictures, the distributors apparently decided there weren't enough monsters in the mash so Johnny actually turned out to be a werewolf! To accomplish this, they filmed some additional scenes of an actor in a Don Post werewolf mask killing a prison guard and chasing a woman through the woods. The new footage doesn't exactly make sense because the werewolf beats the guard to death with a club and in the chase scene he is wearing his prison uniform again even though by this point Johnny has stolen clothes and reached the castle where he apparently keeps a full wardrobe. Later in the film, Johnny doesn't turn into a werewolf during the full moon sacrifice he participates in and is subsequently killed with a regular bullet. These dueling versions kept young horror in fans in arguments for many years depending on who saw what version of the film.

Bloodsucking Freaks(1976)
by Rob St. Mary

Joel M. Reed's 1976 film *Bloodsucking Freaks* (a.k.a. *The Incredible Torture Show*) is one of the few films that is still as notorious today as it was when it was originally released over thirty-five years ago. One of the only other films that meets the same label is Pasolini's *Salo, or the 120 Days of Sodom*. And like *Salo, Bloodsucking Freaks* has things to say that many can't see because they find the surface images too shocking to stomach. In my analysis, Reed's film places female nudity, torture, and dismemberment center stage but is not anti-woman. In fact, the film is a radical pro-feminist statement like something Valerie Solanas (*Scum Manifesto*) could have penned.

Sardu (Seamus O'Brien) is the master of the theater of the macabre—a middle-aged white man who provides the stage for the rest of the characters. Like Sardu, the other main characters are more symbolic than real people be it the ballerina, the cop, the football star, the theater critic, and the henchman. The theater itself can be seen as a microcosm for mid-'70s society, a world where women were dominated by men, made to feel inferior and to do the bidding of the master while having their passions taken away from them if they refuse to conform.

Sardu is an upper-class gentleman. He appreciates the finer things in life—brandy, cigars, and, of course, a little bondage because he's a "bad boy." As a businessman, the theater represents the legitimate face of his operations. The underground aspect is Sardu's sale of young women to the highest bidders worldwide.

Ralphus (Luis de Jesus) is Sardu's Latino dwarf henchman who follows the master's commands in a "Stepin Fetchit" style. Not only in physical stature, but also in the interactions, Ralphus is never equal to the master. As a dwarf, he can symbolize the white supremacist idea that other races are never on equal footing with the white man. Ralphus does the bidding of Sardu by torturing the women to the master's specifications. Sardu is far too dignified to do such things. One could see this as a comment on the place of minorities doing the dirty work in society—from domestics to nannies to waiters and soldiers. The Vietnam War had ended just as *Bloodsucking Freaks* was released and that war saw a huge percentage of African-American soldiers and fatalities.

Maverick (Niles McMaster) is the All-American football hero— a big man in the eyes of other men. Based on 1970s New York Jets quarterback Joe Namath, Maverick is similarly good-looking, charming, and popular. He's a real "man's man" and a "ladies' man." He dates the ballerina Natasha D'Natalie (Viju Krem).

Natasha D'Natalie is a Lincoln Center ballerina kidnapped and forced into Sardu's show. She can be a symbol for most women since her career as a ballerina is often the dream of little girls. Natasha is repulsed by the torture show and refuses to be dominated by Sardu.

Sergeant Tucci (Dan Fauci) is a crooked cop looking for payoffs. Caring less about the laws and ethics, Tucci is an opportunist who plays all sides for his own gain. Tucci can symbolize the cynicism of post-Watergate America. Tucci could also be a stand in for the New York City police department which had just gone through a major corruption scandal a few years earlier.

Creasy Silo (Alan Dellay) is the *New York Times* theater critic. The name is an obvious riff on long time *New York Times* critic Clive Barnes. Silo calls Sardu on his actions. Eventually kidnapped and tortured, Silo's outspoken ways represent an intellectual and enlightened point of view of Sardu's so-called art.

The various tortures in *Bloodsucking Freaks* also work symbolically, highlighting the conforming and containing of female desires on physical, mental, and spiritual levels. For example, in "the iron tourniquet" scene a woman's skull is placed in a metal halo and tightened until her death. One could make the case that the world created by the patriarchy, represented by Sardu, seeks to squeeze the mental power out of women and conform them into a cold, pre-set mold.

Another torture of conformity happens to Natasha. She is brought to Sardu who shows her what will happen if she refuses to dance. Natasha meets another dancer who had her feet cut off. Sardu uses the removal of the means of another woman's way of expressing her passion to motivate Natasha to start rehearsals. The message is clear: do what we tell you or we'll remove your method of expressing your passion in life.

Later in the film a woman is strapped to a table and given electric shocks via her nipples. Nipples can represent motherhood—a place of comfort and feeding as well as sexuality. The torture expresses how society clamps down on woman's sexual passion and expression of motherhood.

But the most obvious metaphor in *Bloodsucking Freaks* is the cage of naked, savage women. One scene in particular is when Sardu calls in a doctor to help nurse Natasha back to health. As payment for his services, the doctor is given a woman to torture. During the scene which involves removing the woman's teeth, shaving her head, and then the infamous "brain-sucking scenes," Sardu tells Ralphus to get rid of the doctor. We get the feeling the doctor may have crossed some sort of unspoken line. This can be seen as an interesting statement on how people on the "same side" philosophically can often times feel like their brothers have gone too far.

After he's done playing Dr. Mengele, the doctor is thrown in with the caged women. They rip him apart. The doctor, a white male in authority, can represent the kind of man society says women should want. But, he placates the caged, passionate women for a short time.

One thing about the world created by Sardu is that women are treated with respect only when they can be used for profit or entertainment. One scene depicting the slave trade finds Ralphus boxing up one of the women for shipment. When she pops out of a box, Ralphus hits her on the head with a mallet and pushes her back in the box. Then he places a "fragile handle with care" sticker on the box. Meaning, once we have properly processed a woman she now has a value because she has been correctly conformed to our society's needs.

While Sardu never tortures any women on stage, in his private life he finds them useful. Sardu uses several as dinner tables, benches, and entertainment. His use of them represents the idea of women as domestic objects with the only real value being how they can serve and please the master while sacrificing their own needs.

The ending of *Bloodsucking Freaks* finds all the symbols together in one giant pro-feminist collage of blood, sex, and death. The final torture show features Natasha dancing and kicking the critic to death because Silo failed to give Sardu artistic respect. So, has Natasha been brainwashed or has she been liberated?

When Maverick finally figures out that his ballerina girlfriend is under the control of Sardu the Svengali, he teams up with Sergeant Tucci. The pair then searches the theater and Tucci ends up in the basement with the caged women, who tear him apart and break free. Once the women are loose, Sardu laughs because he knows his own destruction is imminent. As the caged women exact their revenge, Natasha kills Maverick with a hammer to the back of the head. She then kneels down, tastes his blood, peels off her coat, and runs off naked to join the other women.

As the women dance in freedom, a pan shot reveals the heads of Sardu, Ralphus, and a lone black female henchman. One dancing woman is eating a sandwich. The final shot of the film is a close-up of that sandwich. It's made from a penis. One can infer, since it's white, that it's Sardu's. A penis is the most obvious symbol of a man. The castration and cannibalism can be seen as the women not only fighting the power of the oppressor but completely destroying the system.

Joel M. Reed's film seems to infer a great uprising is coming as the caged passions of women cannot be contained forever. Was Reed trying to make a film speaking to crushing the patriarchy during a time in U.S. History when feminism, the fight for the Equal Rights Amendment, and other women's rights were in on the front pages?

I'm not 100 percent sure.

The film is supposed to be horror sexploitation. But I don't believe one can deny these messages exist within *Bloodsucking Freaks* and, like all great art, it is not overt or preachy. Truly subversive art is often couched in a palatable wrapper. But even that is not the case with *Bloodsucking Freaks*, which has the ability to shock and discomfort. In my view, the great irony of the film is that if the anti-porn feminists would have put down their signs, bought a ticket, and could get past the images to see the symbolism, they might hail the film today as an important statement on the subjugation of women and the battle against patriarchy.

But then again, *Bloodsucking Freaks* is often hard to watch. That's why it is still as notorious today as it was in 1976.

Brainwash (1981)
by Michael Harris

The 1981 film *Brainwash* is what we intellectuals like to call a crazy-ass movie. It begins like an average film in that it introduces the main characters of the story; in this case, several employees of a company called Mystique. These employees are sent to a week-long training course by their employer. This training course is supposed to train these people for moving up the old corporate ladder and being able to better compete for such jobs. Little do they know what is in store for them at the resort-like retreat.

The training course, it turns out, forces these people to confront their worst fears—emotional fears, not things like spiders, lions, staplers, ants, or anything like that. The beautiful and talented Yvette Mimieux plays Bianca Ray, the woman in charge of the facility and the leader of the men's training sessions. You may remember Mimieux as Weena in the 1960 version of *The Time Machine*. The wives of the men who are competing for a higher position within their company are placed in a different set of training sessions with the husband of Bianca Ray. The bulk of the film focuses on the captivating Mimieux and her cruelty towards these men.

The film is not simply about how a woman is cruel to men for her own entertainment, rather it seems to be a criticism of corporate culture and the things people allow themselves to undergo to make more money and gain higher power in their jobs. At the beginning of their training, Bianca has the men form a semicircle in the classroom. The first man she forces to face his fear is made to strip and get into a cage. She humiliates him; however, the result of this is unexpected. In different ways, she makes every man in the group do something humiliating or frightening so as to force each man to confront his fears. By the end of the film, the reason for all of this activity is explained, hence my rationale that this film is anti-corporate world and speaks to the pressures felt by some in said world. This is not a film one would want to watch with impatient movie fans. There are scenes where some may want to yell at the screen and say, "Don't let her do that to you!" The situations presented in the film are not that simple, plus there are big bodyguard dudes in the room anyway, so fighting back wouldn't help them out a whole lot.

Brainwash, a.k.a *Circle of Power*, is a unique film, made during a time of more daring filmmaking, basically 1970 to1985. It probably did not get much of a theatrical release and it is not on DVD. You can find a VHS copy of it on Amazon or eBay from time to time, however. It is worth seeking out and watching because of its no-nonsense approach. Not much time is spent lingering on unimportant nonsense before the primary action of the film takes place. After about ten minutes, we meet Mimieux's character and the fun begins. There is a poster for this film one may find online which shows a woman whose face we cannot see and whose shirt is opened up revealing a bit of breasts, or, as we intellectuals call them, breastages. This is a misleading poster as Mimieux's character is not meant to be a sexual object in the film. She is very sexy; however, the image in that poster has nothing to do with the film.

Brainwash was directed by Bobby Roth, who, according to IMDB, has directed four episodes of the current popular ABC television series *Revenge*. He also directed episodes of *Dr. Quinn Medicine Woman, Prison Break, Lost,* and the short-lived *Flash Forward*. The film does, at first, have the feel of a made-for-TV film. However, its subject matter and some other factors quickly remove all thoughts of Quinn Martin or the old ABC Sunday Night Movie theme.

The reason I like *Brainwash* is fairly simple. I had never seen a film quite like it before. Also, the film's low budget gives it a more intimate feeling—a sense that the viewer is in the training classroom with Mimieux and these men. This makes the film more tangible and without a feeling of isolation from the action. This is one of the probably unintended, though almost always present, aspects of low budget films of the 1970s and 1980s. Because these films were not able to afford a lot of special effects and had to rely on atmosphere, they are sometimes more interesting as long as, of course, the script is decent. I encourage you to seek out this film and not be brain-washed into thinking that just because a film has a low budget and was likely seen at the time as just drive-in fodder, that there is not some substance within that film. Obviously not all low budget films of this time period are good. However, there are quite a few that are worth watching and some great discoveries to be made.

Breaking Point (1975)
by Michael Harris

There are three things which can turn a movie from good to great—a unique storyline, wonderful usage of location shooting, and plenty of female pubic hair.

Breaking Point (1975) has all three of these ingredients. Directed by Bo Arne Vibenius, who also directed the more well-known *Thriller: a Cruel Picture*, *Breaking Point* tells the story of an office worker in Sweden, played by Andreas Bellis—in this film his name is given in the credits as Anton Rothschild—who, in the first five minutes of the film, kills a woman. We do not know why. After that scene, we find that this man has what appears to be a dull job at an office where one of his female co-workers flirts with him by unbuttoning her blouse right in front of his desk. That never happens to me.

At some point during his work day, he walks down to the city subway and sees a beautiful young woman, played by Swedish actress/model Barbara Scott. He follows her to her house and proceeds to ask her to strip. "Strip you," he says to her. She does. They have consensual sex and you realize why the Swedish title of this film is *Pornografik Thriller*. Yep, it has erections, 1970s full frontal nudity…not bad really. This kind of work break is much more fun than sitting in a boring break room eating a candy bar.

Earlier in the film we learn that, because the city has been ravaged with crime against women, the government is giving the population vouchers for free handguns. We learn this from a cool TV report that Rothschild's character and his fellow office workers are watching. You take your voucher to a gun shop and you get your free gun. Of course the crime that sets this government handgun program in motion is the one committed at the beginning of the film by the protagonist played by Mr. Rothschild.

After his dalliance with the subway woman, he goes to a gun shop to claim his government issued handgun. He also has encounters of a sexual nature with two more women, one of whom lives outside the city, so he rents a car to go see her. This is where the wonderful usage of location shooting comes in. I would love to see this film either in a theater or on a re-mastered DVD version. Many scenes were filmed in the Swedish countryside. The opportunity to see mid-70s Swedish city life and the Swedish countryside in the same film is a treat.

Also occurring in the Swedish countryside is the most memorable—but not the best—sex scene in the film. It involves the man's rental car, a very forward woman, and a gear shift. "Not the best one?" you ask. Well, the gear shift does make it a strong second place.

I strongly recommend this film as it creates a fantastic sense of insecurity. I wondered throughout the film, "What will this guy do next?" It is not predictable at all. I love that.

I am sure that a lot of people would find the film offensive and be put off by our lead character's exploits as the film follows him through his mostly sexual dalliances. In between his interesting sexual encounters he takes time, while at home, to masturbate into a coffee cup, take this cup to work with him, and serve coffee in it to the woman who had unbuttoned her shirt in front of his desk—okay, this has to make you want to seek out this film. I was not sure why he did this. However, I was just fine with not understanding his every action during the course of the film. Vibenius seems to be saying to the audience that the lead character's actions will be strange, but enjoy it for what it is. He is not supposed to be a great guy.

It is a wonderful achievement in simplicity and confrontationalism without being confrontational. It asks the audience to watch what this man is doing, but it does not tell the audience what they should be feeling about him or his actions. It is definitely not for the easily offended. However, for those who seek out films that are non-mainstream and disturbing, *Breaking Point* will do its due diligence in being both disturbing and entertaining.

The Candy Tangerine Man (1975)
by David Walker

Even if director Matt Cimber had only made *The Black Six* and the largely forgotten *Lady Cocoa* (a.k.a. *Pop Goes the Weasel*), he would have earned a special place in the hearts of the most diehard blaxploitation fans. While neither film is especially good, both refuse to be absolutely terrible in a way that defines so many other blaxploitation flicks. But it is not *The Black Six* or *Lady Cocoa* that has earned Cimber a special place in the Schlock Cinema Hall of Fame, for neither of those films have the unbridled audacity or pure bravado of *The Candy Tangerine Man*, a movie that puts the "exploit" in exploitation.

Often cited as being Samuel L. Jackson's favorite blaxploitation movie, *The Candy Tangerine Man* is—at least by certain definitions of the term—as classic. A tale of dual identities and one black man's struggle to find financial success in world plagued by systemic racism and limited opportunities, *The Candy Tangerine Man* is a pimp movie unlike any other pimp movie ever made. John Daniels stars as Ron Lewis, a loving husband and father in the suburbs. But at night, Ron Lewis transforms into The Baron, a cold-blooded pimp runnin' ho's and puttin' foot to ass on Los Angeles's Sunset Strip. Between battling the Mafia, keeping the women in his stable in line, dealing with corrupt cops, and making sure his family believes he's a traveling salesman on the road five days out of the week, The Baron has his hands full. In one night alone, The Baron pleasures one of his women, pulls another into his stable, and lays waste to five fools who try to come between him and his game, before returning to his unsuspecting wife, who wants him to fix a busted window in the bathroom. It's a tough life, and as Big Daddy Kane once said,

"Pimpin' ain't easy." But somebody's gotta do it, and The Baron is just the man. Lucky for The Baron he's got a strong pimphand—not to mention his pimpmobile, outfitted with machine guns hidden behind the headlights. In fact he's more than a pimp, he's the Candy Tangerine Man—a super pimp, with pimpabilities far beyond those of mortal pimps.

By the time this film was released in 1975, the blaxploitation cycle had pretty much been played out. A political backlash that began in 1972 surrounding the film *Super Fly* charged that most of the films being produced for black audiences focused on morally suspect characters and glorified black criminality. Organizations like the NAACP and CORE took issue with movies like *Super Fly* and *The Mack*, but the vast majority of all blaxploitation films were pretty tame when held up next to *The Candy Tangerine Man*. If, in fact, any of the movies produced during the blaxploitation era were worthy of harsh criticism for being morally corrupt and pandering to the exploitative elements of sex and violence, it is this film. If there was ever a film that could be described as depraved grindhouse swill—in the most positive of contexts, mind you—it would have to be *The Candy Tangerine Man*. The film contains everything from golden showers to rape to mutilation (one hooker gets her breasts cut off and a mob enforcer loses a hand in a garbage disposal). And of course there is the cast of extras, which, according to the credits, features "the actual hookers and blades of Sunset Strip in Hollywood," all of whom lend an air of authenticity to the movie, while also being some of the most unattractive people captured on film.

John Daniels gives what is arguably the finest performance of his career as Ron Lewis/The Baron. Daniels is best known by blaxploitation fans for this film and director Greydon Clark's mind-melting sleazefest *Black Shampoo*. Daniels also appeared in such films as *Hit Man* (the blaxploitation remake of *Get Carter*), *Bare Knuckles*, and *Getting Over* (which he co-wrote and co-produced). Outside of film, Daniels was a successful businessman, magazine publisher, song writer, nightclub owner, and manager of the all-women singing group The Love Machine. His Los Angeles nightclub, Maverick's Flat, is a place of legend, having played host to some of the greatest R&B and funk acts of all time. Acting was never Daniels's greatest passion, which is fortunate, since he has a rather limited range. But his limited skills as an actor are not so much a reflection of whatever talent he may or may not have possessed, but rather an indictment on the work of director Matt Cimber.

Having already established that the crafting of fine cinematic fare was not his strong point, Cimber sticks to what he does best with *The Candy Tangerine Man*. And what he does best is craft low budget exploitation flicks meant to offer momentary distraction from the outside world. In the smoke-filled grindhouse theaters, and at the drive-in theaters that showed movies like *The Candy Tangerine Man* sandwiched in with other movies as part of double and triple features, the standards of determining good from bad are always in flux. *The Candy Tangerine Man* is one of those films that walk the line between sleazy and charming, and to be perfectly honest, it takes a special person to appreciate that fine line. That's not to say the film is not worth watching, or even enjoying with a sort of sadistic, depraved pleasure, because if that's your cup of tea, then this cup runneth over. By the stick used to measure movies of this nature, *The Candy Tangerine Man* is a good film. Of course, "good" is a purely subjective standard that must be applied accordingly.

Cannibal Holocaust (1980)
by Shannon L. Grisso

Ruggero Deodato's *Cannibal Holocaust* is one of those rare films that manages to live up to its reputation. What is surprising, though, is that it not only lives up to its good reputation as a grueling, intense horror film, but also *down* to its reputation as an indefensible and misanthropic movie.

The Italian cannibal cycle began in 1972 with Umberto Lenzi's *Man from Deep River* and only lasted until the end of the decade, when titles such as Lenzi's *Eaten Alive, Mondo Canibale,* and *The Devil Hunter* glutted the market in 1980.

The one cannibal film which still manages to generate the most controversy and debate, even among the hardcore blood and guts crowd, is Ruggero Deodato's amazing *Cannibal Holocaust.* Much like *The Texas Chain Saw Massacre, Pink Flamingos,* or even *Caligula*, it's one of those films you just have to see, if only to figure out what all the fuss is about.

The story is very simple: an anthropology professor (played by porn regular Robert Kerman) undertakes an expedition to the Amazon jungle in search of a missing film crew. That film crew had ventured into the jungle to produce a documentary on two warring cannibal tribes and, after meeting with one of the tribes, the professor discovers a bunch of exposed film in film cans adorning the skeletons of the missing film crew. Once back in the States, the professor is shown the film that was shot by the crew and learns of their awful (if fully deserved) fate.

The first half of the film is a little slow, and may even lull the first-time viewer into thinking that maybe this movie doesn't deserve its controversy. Once we get to the "found footage," though, we are presented with some truly astounding, disturbing, grisly and stunning imagery. What makes this footage even more shocking, however, are two tricks employed by the director that manage to plant the idea in the back of the viewer's mind that what he is seeing might be "real."

First, at about the midway point (but before we are shown any of the "found footage"), we are shown a clip from a previous film made by the documentary crew. Titled *The Long Road to Hell*, it is little more than footage of men, women, and children being shot and killed. This footage, culled from numerous Mondo films, is absolutely authentic and disturbing.

Then we have the most controversial aspect of *Cannibal Holocaust*—its animal violence. We see a muskrat get the top of its head sliced off, a turtle gutted and hacked to pieces, a snake chopped up, and a tethered pig kicked and shotgunned. In light of today's politically correct environment, these images seem so far removed from anything we can relate to that they go beyond shocking and almost immediately numb the viewer. When taken together with the use of real death footage in the *Long Road* segment, that thought is placed snugly in the back of your mind: "if all of this is real, I wonder if anything else is…?"

Real or not, the violence in the second half of *Cannibal Holocaust* achieves astounding levels, culminating in a brutal rape and concurrent murder that surely cannot have been intended for entertainment purposes. In fact, that is the key to this film: instead of being a fun, carnival ride kind of horror film with escalating gross-out set pieces, this is not "fun"—it's intended only to sledgehammer and brutalize the viewer. The repeated, blunt, "real" (or faked, but seemingly real) violent moments combine to produce a film that will linger in the memory long after it has been viewed.

Is it a metaphor for and condemnation of the media's exploitation of violence for violence's sake, or is it merely an example *of* violence for violence's sake? In reality, it is both and successful in each.

This is also one of those films with so many rumors and legends around it that it is nearly impossible to know which are true and which are mere folklore. While there are many sensationalistic claims that the film was banned in over fifty different countries, it is true that it was seized and banned in the country of its origin (Italy) barely a week after it was released. The film remained banned there for nearly three years and Deodato faced charges of violating a law prohibiting the killing of animals for purposes of entertainment. Supposedly, Deodato had the actors playing the documentary crew agree to drop out of sight for a full year, so they could more fully suggest that their deaths were genuine; this tactic backfired when the same Italian courts demanded he produce them to ensure they were not actually killed on screen. Interestingly, one of the actors comments on the film's IMDB page that when he showed up in the jungle he was a bit uncertain as to whether or not he'd wandered into the making of an actual snuff movie.

Perhaps the best way to prove that *Cannibal Holocaust* is one of those lightning rod, controversial films is to point out my own personal dealings with it. Since seeing it nearly fifteen years ago, on a bootlegged VHS from a Japanese laserdisc, I have been fascinated with the film, both for its own merits and for the effect it has on myself and others. The soundtrack (reissued in a beautiful digi-pak from Season of Mist) is beautiful and tragic, and is in fact on my iPod right now (I like to fall asleep to it).

It's also one of the most viewed films in my collection. Whenever I invite someone over to watch a couple of movies, I let them go through my DVD collection and choose whatever they would like to watch, and—no lie—the single most requested title in my personal library is *Cannibal Holocaust* (the second, oddly enough, is *Kiss Meets the Phantom of the Park*).

This really bothers my wife, a confirmed animal lover who absolutely detests the fact that I own the movie in the first place. It's also one of a very select few movies that I have to watch either when she is in another room, asleep, or out of the house altogether (and heaven forbid if she enters the room and I do not promptly turn it off until she leaves again).

Two more amusing anecdotes come from my experiences in my job at a video store (yes, there are a few of those left out there). I knew of the Grindhouse Releasing DVD months in advance, and had a copy on special order. It arrived on a day when I was not at work and a customer, spotting it on the shelf, offered the video manager a little extra money if he would sell him my copy out from under me. Thankfully, he refused. Years later I overheard a bunch of teenagers discussing the horror movies we offered for rent. One of the group noticed *Cannibal Holocaust*, and another kid excitedly gushed about what a horrible and offensive film it was. He described the animal violence in detail, told the others to never watch it, then said he might rent it himself just so he could scratch it up and prevent anyone else from ever renting it again. At that point I advised him it probably wouldn't be a good idea for him to do that, and we had a friendly debate about the film. (By the way, he did not in fact ruin the movie—we still have it at my store for rental.)

But probably my favorite anecdote concerns when I showed it to my brother. Although interested in extreme cinema, he is not nearly as jaded a filmgoer as I. One night, after a few drinks, he decided he'd heard enough about *Cannibal Holocaust* and decided he'd take a chance on it. He was pretty disturbed by it all, and we discussed it for a little while before calling it a night. The next day while I was at work, he decided to watch it again to see if it really was as disturbing as he'd thought, or if it was just the combination of the movie and the alcohol. This time around, watching it stone cold sober, he was unable to make it all the way to the end.

And that pretty much says it all. *Cannibal Holocaust* is hard to describe, difficult to recommend, and impossible to defend. Love it or hate it, it's just one of those legendary movies you simply have to see for yourself.

You have been warned...

Children Shouldn't Play with Dead Things (1973)
by E.D. Tucker

By the early 1970s, *Night of the Living Dead* was already well on its way to becoming a cult classic, and audiences all across the country were eating up this new zombie film. Two of those audience members were aspiring director Bob Clark and writer Alan Ormsby. The duo had raised funds from friends and relatives for a low-budget motion picture and had just found the inspiration they were seeking. Realizing the potential that *Night* had created and acknowledging Ormsby's love of horror films, Clark decided they should produce a similar genre title. Working at top speed, Bob Clark had a rough script ready to go within a few weeks and the black comedy/zombie horror film *Children Shouldn't Play with Dead Things* was born.

Bob Clark had already directed a few obscure films in south Florida by the time he and Alan Ormsby met, but he was ready for something he had more control over. Both men were willing to do whatever was needed to get their breakout film on the screen and that was just what this movie would require. While Clark oversaw all aspects of the production, with help from friend Gary Goch, Ormsby contributed to the script, designed the more complicated make-up effects, and even played the lead character. The remaining cast was made up of friends, relatives, and members of the University of Miami drama department.

Children Shouldn't Play with Dead Things is the story of an aspiring acting troupe and their domineering leader played by Ormsby, also named Alan. At his behest, they travel to a small island off the coast of Florida for an intensive training workshop without distractions. This retreat also includes a nasty practical joke and a seemingly unsuccessful voodoo ritual, most likely designed to unnerve the actors and further assert their leader's control. Egos, however, are about to be the least of these "Children's" problems.

As part of the ritual to raise the dead, the corpse of recently-deceased Orville Dunworth is exhumed and hung on a crucifix. Following the failure of the ceremony and the general disbelief of his troupe, Alan has the body brought back with them to their cabin so it can undergo further indignities. After a sacrilegious marriage and various taunting, Orville is put through the most degrading ordeal imaginable when he is forced to listen to Alan's self-absorbed introspective contemplations. It's completely believable that drivel like this could cause the dead to turn in their graves and eventually rise!

For the final act, the film switches tone abruptly from black comedy to straight horror. The ghouls from the local cemetery claw their way to the surface in some effectively atmospheric scenes and then begin wiping out the cast in short order. The cabin standoff is very reminiscent of *Night of the Living Dead*, but is wisely kept brief in favor of a futile escape attempt and a downbeat ending where Orville gets a little payback on his chief defiler.

The first hour of *Children Shouldn't Play with Dead Things* is a slow-paced setup to an enjoyable climax. With such a leisurely beginning, you would think there would be more explanation of the relationships of the characters but very little is given. Most frustrating is the lack of a clear reason why the "Children" are following a jerk like Alan in the first place. He does not appear to be their stepping stone to acting careers and the satanic ritual implies a certain Manson-like devotion that is also never explored. Thankfully, by the final reel the film does deliver the horror the audience has been waiting for. The zombie makeup is a mixed variety that gives the impression of different stages of decomposition for the corpses. The gore is restricted to some free-flowing blood, but nothing approaching the *Night of the Living Dead* scale. Even for a PG-rated film of the 1970s, the film seems to shy away from anything too explicit which may be due to Bob Clark's dislike of the horror genre.

The most memorable aspect of this film is the atmosphere, thanks to some interesting locations and odd lighting. The majority of the shooting was done at the Dade County Nursery which provides a foliage-covered graveyard and a nearby ramshackle house that one of the crew members actually lived in at the time and rented to the production. The lighting setups were courtesy of local cinematographer Jack McGowan, who was a well-respected member of the Florida film scene. Hand held lanterns and disembodied street lights are combined with fog and colored gels to give the film an unsettling, nightmare-like quality that sticks with the viewer.

Children had a lengthy theatrical release courtesy of Ted V. Mikels' Gemini Film Distributors, including at least one re-release on a triple bill under the more direct title *Revenge of the Living Dead*. From there it headed into television syndication and proved popular on late night and horror-themed movie programs (including the 44 *Creature Feature*). In the mid-80s, the film was picked up for the newly created home video market and spent the next decade in easy access on store shelves thanks to a variety of different video labels.

Following this film, Clark would go on to a very prosperous career in directing, including the teen comedy *Porky's* and the modern holiday classic *A Christmas Story.* Ormsby concentrated on writing and penned the scripts for the *Cat People* remake and the highly-underrated *My Bodyguard* as well as many television shows. Most of the remaining cast either stuck close to the Clark/Ormsby partnership for the next few years or faded into obscurity. Two notable exceptions were Jan Daly, who played Terry, and has worked steadily, mainly in television, ever since and Jeff Gillen, who would make a memorable cameo in *A Christmas Story* as the grumpy store Santa who pushes young Ralphie down the slide with his foot!

While it may not have come close to the level of the film that inspired it, *Children Shouldn't Play with Dead Things* did develop its own cult following and is still a favorite among many horror fans today. According to Alan Ormsby, the film was successful enough at the box office for a sequel, tentatively titled *We Told You... Children Shouldn't Play with Dead Things*, to enter the planning stages but it never went any further. Instead, Clark and Ormsby collaborated on two more horror films, the eerie anti-war movie *Death Dream* and the Ed Gein-inspired *Deranged.* Following the recent commercial success and critical failure of the remake of Clark's *Black Christmas*, the director was in serious talks on a remake of *Children* at the time of his tragic death in an automobile accident that also claimed the life of his son. While a remake is still a possibility given the recycling frenzy in Hollywood these days, until then fans can continue to enjoy the quirky original.

Compass Rose (1967)
by Rob Craig

Just as one man's "trash" is another man's treasure, so is today's "lost" film tomorrow's commonplace. Such is the case with *Compass Rose*, one of the earliest sexploitation films made by New York-based iconoclast Andy Milligan. As is hopefully common knowledge to anyone reading this book, Andy Milligan (1929-1991) was a filmmaker who made over thirty completely unique sexploitation and horror melodramas. Many of these wonderfully lurid and primitive films were shot in New York or London, on minuscule budgets, in grainy 16mm film, with an old newsreel camera; a few later films were shot via 35mm in sunny California. Much of Milligan's early output was released by Times Square grindhouse legend William Mishkin, and played to considerable box-office (if not critical) success at countless drive-ins and skid-row hard-tops around the country before being abandoned.

Several of Milligan's horror titles, including the infamous *The Ghastly Ones* (1968) and *Bloodthirsty Butchers* (1970), eventually found their way to home video, and are fairly easy to access in various home viewing formats. Yet for many years, virtually all of Milligan's sexploitation films were considered lost, including: *The Promiscuous Sex, The Naked Witch, The Filthy Five, Gutter Trash, Kiss Me! Miss Me! Kiss Me!, The Degenerates, Depraved, Nightbirds* and *Compass Rose*. Yet such are the vagaries of the collector's marketplace that one existing print of *Nightbirds* (purportedly Milligan's own personal print) turned up on online auction site eBay awhile back and was purchased by filmmaker Nicolas Winding Refn. With the help of the British Film Institute, he remastered the film print and released it on DVD—to much adoration and acclaim.

A much more low-key, yet still laudable, fate lay in store for Milligan's 1967 melodrama *Compass Rose*, which turned up unceremoniously one day on a "bit torrent" site on the world wide web. The as-yet anonymous donor of *Compass Rose* is owed a great debt of gratitude for procuring and uploading what is undoubtedly one of few—if not the only—print of this earliest incarnation of the Milligan sexploitation canon.

Regardless of the film's content, the resurrection of *Compass Rose* would surely be cause for celebration, but finally viewing this extremely primitive effort (even by Milligan standards) is a joy to any true trash-film and/or Milligan fan. *Compass Rose* is an impressive, if almost comically lurid, sexually-tinged "kitchen sink" melodrama of the old school, boasting many of the characters, motifs and themes which would appear with shocking regularity in subsequent Milligan productions. These cherished Milligan tropes include: a severely dysfunctional family, peopled with unstable neurotics who always seem poised to lurch into psychosis; endless bickering and fighting amongst these hapless relatives; unbridled lust which veers always towards the violent; bitter, hyper-theatrical diatribes by one or more characters regarding how their loved ones have horrifically betrayed their trust. These calculatedly over-the-top histrionics are filmed by Milligan's often hand-held camera in a wildly unschooled style, quite similar to that of underground filmmakers of the day, including Andy Warhol, Paul Morrissey, Curtis Harrington, Kenneth Anger, and Jack Smith, art-film legends with which the neglected grind-house impresario shares a great deal. Shot in claustrophobic, even gloomy real-life locations with tinny sound and deep shadows creating an almost unbearable primitivism, *Compass Rose* looks like a home movie shot in an insane asylum by one of the more creatively-inclined inmates, who tossed a script at his halfway-house fellows and shouted, "Act, dammit, act!"

Compass Rose takes place entirely in lower Manhattan, and includes some amazing exterior scenes of Greenwich Village circa 1967. The story haphazardly follows a gaggle of Gotham flotsam through several parties, traumas and even an orgy; these include a male hustler, an aging movie star, assorted junkies and whores, and some outrageously flaming gays. As such it captures—probably fairly faithfully—a cross-section of the actual demographic of the

Beat scene of the day, with ostentatious nods to the Warhol Factory crowd and the Off-Off Broadway crowd, groups with which Milligan was intimately familiar. In fact, several of Milligan's compatriots from the infamous Caffe Cino appear in *Compass Rose*, verifying that he had already gathered many of the stock players which he would use faithfully in later films.

Several narrative tropes in *Compass Rose* reappear in later Milligan works. The most conspicuous is a house-call by a creepy doctor and nurse, who administer a blood transfusion to an ailing elderly woman, a scene repeated almost intact in *Seeds of Sin*, and resurrected with minor variation in *Bloodthirsty Butchers* and *The Body Beneath*. Another conspicuous parallel between *Compass Rose* and *Seeds of Sin*, other than the similar cast and interior setting, is the appearance in both of Candy Hammond—Milligan's then-wife—as a neurotic floozy who masturbates, topless, on her bed. These and other similarities suggest that the two films were filmed simultaneously or in close sequence.

One may be surprised to find that the film's title is not a character's name, but the deus ex machina of the haphazard narrative. In nautical terms, a compass rose is an instrument which tells the seafaring traveler in which direction he goes, attempting to align his voyage with true north, that unassailable point on which all successful voyages ultimately rely. Here, the term is used twice by the leading matriarch, once at the film's start and again at the end, to forewarn that without a reliable ethical anchor or moral compass, man is lost, to become awash in a sea of meaningless depravity which will ultimately drown him. This arch-conservative viewpoint is, of course, a prevalent theme throughout all of Milligan's films, so it is exciting to find it in full force in one of his earliest works.

The big finale takes place on the opening night of a particularly obnoxious play at a local off-Broadway dive. The play is so ridiculous and pretentious it comes across as a mockery of the genre, another curious act of loathing by Milligan towards his own community. Also quite mean-spirited is a short trip to a psychedelic hippie commune, where sad burn-outs sway in drugged-out ecstasy and chant "Hare Rama, Hare Krishna" ad infinitum. Award-winning playwright Robert Patrick gives a stunning over-the-top performance as a consumptive junkie playwright and spouts one of the film's best lines: "We're all stars, honey, and we're looking for a vehicle...someone to ride!" Among many unnerving later scenes is one in which the Candy Hammond character kills herself by sticking a pistol in her mouth, a sexually-tinged act of self-violence which was brought to gruesome mainstream life a few years later in Russ Meyer's extraordinary *Beyond the Valley of the Dolls* (1970).

The final bombshell in this always-surprising film occurs at the film's end. Miss Gloria, the woman who now feels betrayed by her gigolo, summons a band of man-hating lesbians to slowly torture him to death. The infantile, knee-jerk misandry of this ludicrous comic-book gang of dyke thugs whipping the poor sap into oblivion says a great deal about Milligan, scenarist Josef Bush, and the culture of the times, in which the empowered female collective ("woman's libbers") were demonized (by some) as violent separatist enemies of male society.

Compass Rose is an exciting discovery for many reasons, including that it is the narrative "missing link" between Milligan's inaugural effort, the underground art-film *Vapors* (ca 1965), and his subsequent grindhouse sexploitation movies. Indeed, *Compass Rose* rides the fence conspicuously between art-film and commercial film, containing abundant elements of both genres, suggesting that Milligan was feeling his way towards the commercial grindhouse skin-flick game with this extraordinary early effort. Indeed, as the main character in *Compass Rose* is a male hustler, one wonders if Andy Warhol's *My Hustler* (1965) was an inspiration for this most curious take on same—and if Warhol and Paul Morrissey's smash hit *Trash* (1970) borrowed the essential narrative arc of *Compass Rose*? The extant copy of *Compass Rose* appears to be from an unfinished work print, as there are no titles or credits of any kind, several almost indecipherable dialogue exchanges, and no music or sound effects. Thus, it is fascinating to see a Milligan film in an almost pure state, as it was likely taken from his 16mm newsreel camera. One wonders if this print is the original (and possibly only) one in existence, making this remarkable film even more of an art-house treasure deserving to be preserved. As they say, one man's trash...

Cut Throats Nine (1972)
by C. Courtney Joyner

A blade cuts into a wide belly, followed by an eruption of blood. Muscle and flesh hang on the knife as it's pulled out and plunged in again. A woman's hysterical scream carries over the image, echoing, and staying with us well into the next shots of director Joaquin Luis Romero Marchent's *Cut Throats Nine*.

It's one of many vivid, savage, revolting moments from a Spanish import that was first perceived as having no artistic, and slight commercial, purpose. Released in 1973 with a pure trash ad campaign, *Cut Throats Nine* entered the American marketplace as less than a bill-filler, but exploited as a gore-fest it secured some box office dollars.

In the years since, *Cut Throats* has become, because of Marchent's own dramatic truths, a respected cult film that just happens to be the ultimate western-horror movie.

The first time I experienced it, my head was left swimming. I knew I kind of liked it, but wasn't sure why. It made me drink, and think. The sadistic violence splattered across me with a different kind of impact than the outlaw shoot-outs and slow motion death-ballets I loved, so *Cut Throats* was definitely a western, but with the bleakest view of the human condition I'd seen outside of a documentary.

The film struck a chord, and I couldn't escape it. *Cut Throats Nine* was surely a western, but it was also genuine horror. Human horror. The poster promised something that the movie delivered, but the film has more brains in its intent than are blown all over the screen.

Much has been made of the film's combination of Fulci-like violence amid a frontier story of escaped convicts, but this comparison is faulty. The savagery of the Spanish-produced *Cut Throats* pre-dates the Euro zombie craze by years and it was the influence of American westerns, rather than Euro horror, that inspired Marchent.

The history behind that inspiration and Marchent's achievement goes back to a time before movies talked.

The trappings of the western and horror first collided on film in silent serials and quickies, like 1926's *The Haunted Range.* By the 1930s, Gower Gulch westerns regularly gave us masked phantoms that haunted gold mines and old train yards before being debunked by a young John Wayne or an aging Hoot Gibson.

The mixture was an easy one to exploit since producers saw the genres as coexisting, appealing to the same audience: youngsters and yokels. When Universal released their last monster rally, *House of Dracula*, in 1945, they paired it with *The Daltons Ride Again*, both starring Lon Chaney.

Monsters 'n cowboys on the same bill, what kid wouldn't love that?

But movies began to change.

Post World War II America was a brightly lit place of victory and home. It was also a shadowed and venomous pit, where the American psyche was twisting in on itself, and movies were our mirror.

The safe haven of old-fashioned monster-horror was now fodder for Abbott and Costello, and the stalwart western hero now seemed quaint. As the gangster film became *film noir*, so the western had moved in darker directions since the war.

Directors Raoul Walsh (*Pursued*), Henry Hathaway (*Rawhide*), and William Wellman (*Yellow Sky*), tackled stories with a cynical, tougher view of the frontier. It was no longer a land of unending promise, but, like the city streets, a harsh landscape populated by troubled heroes and bad men who could be dangerously unbalanced.

Even the One-Eyed Titan's approach was becoming less romantic, less hopeful and, finally, beautifully acid, as John Ford let his personal darkness pour out of him in *My Darling Clementine* and *Wagonmaster.* Ford's villains weren't old-school "side-winders," but slobbering, in-bred psychopaths that could only be controlled by a whip and a .12 gauge. No horror movie torture chamber ever housed anything worse than these creatures.

The band of desperate fugitives in Marchent's *Cut Throats* could rightfully be the cinematic grandchildren of the Clantons and

Cleggs in Ford's two masterful films, with *Cut Throat's* tone as bleak as Ford's darkest moods.

Without realizing it, Ford brought the horror and western genres together in a mature, visual way by turning his west into a shadowed, gothic trap, and his villains into subhumans, waiting for the chance to rape and kill.

We can imagine the impact this new approach had on the young Marchent, a true western devotee who was preparing to direct his first feature. Having grown up under the clamp of the Franco regime, Marchent treasured every rare chance to see American movies, always returning to see the great, "traditional" westerns.

He worked in studios in Madrid as an assistant director before striking out on his own in 1953 with the crime drama, *Juzgado Permanente (Court of Justice)*. When he directed *El Coyote* and a sequel in 1955, starring Abel Salazar, Marchent was now working in his beloved genre, making a western with a masked hero modeled after Zorro.

El Coyote made Marchent perfect to helm new Zorro adventures and in 1962, after two sly comedies, he made *Zorro, The Avenger* and *Shades of Zorro*, both written by his frequent collaborator, Jess Franco, and starring Frank Lattimore.

The Zorro films were well made and sold directly to American television with little regard or respect. But they'd found a place in the U.S. Market, which meant success for the Spanish productions, giving Marchent the chance to make more westerns.

During the 50s, the genre had exploded, with John Wayne riding herd on the box office well into the next decade, followed by Stewart, Cooper, Lancaster, and company. But in 1964, the international market was about to change it all with the atomic success of TV star Clint Eastwood and Sergio Leone's collaboration, signaling the dominance of the Euro-western. The world took notice, turning star and director into icons.

But Jose Marchent had gotten there first, making a pair of Spanish-German productions a full year before *Fistful of Dollars* that are now considered the first true Euro-westerns.

Starring muscleman Richard Harrison, *Gunfight at High Noon* (*El Sabor de la Vengaza*) is the story of three brothers who follow separate paths to track down the man who killed their father twenty years before.

Marchent wrote and directed with an eye on the contrast of the brothers who consider all options before violence against the one who is a blood-in-the-eye gunman, killing all who get in his way. This theme would carry into *Cut Throats Nine*, by examining the men who hunger for violence, equating revenge with justice, and those who don't.

In *Gunfight*, that moral difference sets the brothers at each other, not just the man they're hunting. As in *Cut Throats*, even the good die bloody; there's no escape from violent death in Marchent's west.

Made the same year, *Hour of Death* (*Antes Llega la Muerte*) has been cited as Marchent's masterpiece. Others find its story of the frontier settlers too slow; its concentration on character instead of violence off-putting. The film actually has a high body count, but Marchent is clearly influenced by Ford's *Wagonmaster*, and this was his attempt at that classical style and pace, with bursts of violence that aren't nearly as shocking as in Ford's film. *Hour of Death* is certainly sentimental as it shows the pioneer struggle against the elements and the Indians. It's a triumph of atmosphere and feeling, and displays another side of the director's talents. But like *Gunfight*, the film was hurried off to American television and quickly forgotten while *Fistful* and Corbucci's *Django* launched hundreds of new productions and new fortunes.

But the Spanish master of the form wasn't included in the gold rush. Marchent continued making quality westerns with Spanish content, but the films were shuffled a lot, with flashes of action, but no fanfare. He was now just another working director, making films for an international marketplace that was already stuffed with western movies.

Joaquin Marchent hadn't directed a film in four years (1968's *I Do Not Forgive—I Kill!*) when he began production on *Condenados a Vivir*, with locations in the Pyrenees Mountains and interiors in Madrid. An all-Spanish production made for a small budget, Marchent was working from a brutal screenplay he'd fashioned with Mario Bava collaborator Santiago Moncada (*Hatchet for the Honeymoon*) that emphasized the human emotion of horrific violence instead of straight western action.

The genre had become a violent playground since Peckinpah's *The Wild Bunch* in 1969 and taken a savage turn in films like Ralph

Nelson's 1970 *Soldier Blue*, showing the brutalization of Native Americans by the Army. But Marchent wasn't interested in an epic exaggeration, something he couldn't afford anyway, or the politics of violence. In *Cut Throats* violence is indifferent; a bullet or knife has no allegiance.

The scenario of *Cut Throats* is deceptively simple: an army sergeant is transporting a group of dangerous prisoners to a fort when their wagon is attacked, and the prisoners escape, taking the sergeant and his daughter hostage. What the condemned men don't know is the trip's other purpose—carrying a fortune in gold that's been forged into the chains shackling them together.

The psychotic band kills the sergeant, rapes the daughter, and turn on each other for the gold, leaving a pile of corpses. The mentally destroyed daughter kills the rest, and herself, with dynamite.

"Fin."

Using a classic journey structure for its story, like Ford or Hawks's *Red River*, Marchent's structure allows him to hang his moments of horror on the story's spine. The characters are in motion, trying to reach their goals of the fort, and then freedom, and, finally, riches. And we are always moving with them, watching as they actually take their steps toward bloody death.

Marchent chose his frequent star Robert Hundar (a.k.a. Claudio Undari) as the good sergeant. Hundar's presence is solid and sincere, and he brings authority to the part, even if seeming a tad too young. Undari had first worked with Marchent on *Zorro* in 1962. Emma Cohen has the most difficult part, in that it's hard to justify her character being along on this mission with her father, except that she has nowhere to go after the death of her mother at the hands of one of the cut throats—a fact she never discovers.

Cohen bundles herself and her body together, eyes cast down, trying to distance herself from the prisoners before she is brutally raped by them, and her father slaughtered. Then she is numb, stumbling along with the men as their prisoner, until she takes her own life and theirs. This is a fine performance, with complicated layers that she plays very well, even when implausible.

But the daughter is the feminine voice of the film and, ultimately, the angel of death. We have seen astonishing violence against women by the film's final scenes and it's only fitting that Cohen destroy the destroyers.

Cohen had already been seen in Jess Franco's *Count Dracula*, and after *Cut Throats* would make *Horror Rises from the Tomb*, one of the Spanish horrors from the period mostly widely seen on television.

Unlike the typical Euro-western at the time, where multiple money sources often dictated international casting, the Spanish production money behind *Cut Throats* meant drawing exclusively on Spanish talent. This could have been a handicap, but Marchent's cast has an expansive background. These were the familiar, pockmarked faces from Spanish western, gangster, and horror movies, providing one more link between *Cut Throats* and other genres.

And that link is as strong as the chain that binds the prisoners. Marchent creates a classic western story framework, feeding into typical audience expectations, and then blows a bloody hole right through it with the scenes of violence for which the film is now infamous.

The first moment, after outlaws attack the prison wagon, is a bloodless sniping of a soldier, followed by a rifle butt smashing open another's skull and, moments later, a throat being slit.

Marchent takes each moment of violence further than the one before it. Corpse burnings, stabbings, shootings, disemboweling, and savage beatings come one atop the other, each more startling than the last, as Marchent bloodies the snow along the mountain trails.

But his camera never wavers. The scene of a wagon tumbling over a hillside startles us, not because of flashy stunt work, but because it's presented as plainly as news footage of a car accident.

Marchent and cameraman Luis Cuadrado (*Spirit of the Bee Hive*) maintain a focused, naturalistic eye on the action, allowing the bloody violence to impact us on its own, as if we were standing next to it, without flourish. The background is frozen and blue, with all of the horrible actions of the characters in contrast to its cold and stillness.

When director and cameraman do allow warm colors and soft focus, it's in the film's flashbacks. As in Leone's *Duck, You Sucker*, these are romantic, hazy images of life before prison, when each man had his freedom or was happy with his family. But we're fools to be lulled into enjoyment. The flashbacks ultimately contain some of the movie's nastiest moments, including the back of a woman's head being blown off and the death of the sergeant's wife. Visually, the soft flashbacks allow us a breather, but there's no escape from Marchent's vision and in a heartbeat he's rubbing our noses in the horror. Again.

And all of this builds to the rape scene.

This is *Cut Throats*'s most horrifying moment, because it is real, violent, and ugly. This isn't a hot babe being mauled by a guy in a suit; this is a defenseless woman being treated like an animal. Again, Marchent goes for real horror, real emotion. And it leaves us, like Emma Cohen's character, numb.

The journey of the group continues, with the sergeant dead, his daughter lost in her mind, and the bunch turning on each other. When the prisoners decide to free themselves of their shackles by letting a train run over the chains, it brings home the reality of what Marchent was dealing with as a filmmaker: there is no train, only shadows and a blurred impression of wheels, because there was no money. It's a damn clever sequence, but it points up the film's low budget, and the struggles of its director, who should have had access to more money, more time, and more prestige.

Cut Throats's final moments are the boiling point. More death, as what's left of the gang savages itself and the one outlaw that Emma Cohen has found solace with is brutally taken out. When he is killed, she has no idea who he really was.

In the final irony, she uses dynamite to revenge a man who murdered her mother, finally wiping the bloody, chilled landscape clean. She has killed herself, destroyed the gold, and the last of the cut throats in a blast and fireball. And the image freezes, the cabin blown to smithereens, the snow-covered mountains behind it. Nothing man-made remains.

Marchent's statement is over, and we're left battered by the journey, just as he intended, but distributors saw something else. Something to bring in some quick bucks.

"An adventure in violence that will rip your heart out!" was how American International trumpeted the film when they gave it its spotty release. Looking at it strictly as a gore flick, they gave out "Terror Masks" for patrons who were too chicken-hearted to see all that Joaquin Marchent had wrought.

It played out its week and then it was gone, washed away with the last of the Euro-westerns. Joaquin Marchent continued working in Spain, primarily on television, with no marked success in the United States. He died in Madrid in 2012 at the age of 92, knowing that his most notorious movie now had a cult reputation, not just for horror fans, but western fans who finally gave him rightful credit for his achievements.

Is his most famous film a western? Yes, with a style crafted by someone who loved and understood the genre. Horror? Absolutely, but drawing on different sources than old genre crossovers like *Curse of the Undead*.

Cut Throats is a brutal and real experience, with more impact than Adrian Hoven's *Mark of the Devil* or other "gore notorious" films from the time that used the background of satanic worship of witch-finding atrocities as an excuse for naked girls and tons of blood.

There's nothing supernatural here, no dramatic "out." The horror of *Cut Throats* is the lengths people will go to for riches or revenge. And we're chained right along with them, marching through the snow, ready for bloody death.

Cut Throats Nine has been announced for remaking, starring Harvey Keitel, which may be the ultimate testament to the movie's reputation.

Joaquin Marchent was a fine director who, later in a career that hadn't brought him worldwide success, made the trek into the mountains, with little money, to make the most brutal western ever.

With limited resources he did this and more, creating the ultimate western-horror film that at its heart isn't exploitation, but an exploration of the darkest side of the human experience.

Using the westerns that he loved as inspiration, Marchent succeeded in creating true horror.

Cyclone (1978)
by David C. Hayes

Rene Cardona, Jr. The name alone inspires apathy throughout the film community. And that is truly a shame. Cardona, following in the footsteps of his director father, Rene Cardona, Sr. of course, has crafted a directing resume that is three decades old and is populated with over 90 feature films. Yet, not a soul can put a face to the near legendary Mexploitation master. Maybe it is due solely to marketing? If Tim Burton had cast Johnny Depp as Rene Cardona, Jr., and not Ed Wood, maybe midnight screenings of schlock classics like *Cyclone* and *Tintorera* would grace the screens of theaters everywhere. As far as filmmaking skill goes, both Wood and Cardona are in the same league. Stock footage, reused footage and self-referential dialogue (in *Cyclone*, the characters actually refer to Cardona Sr.'s *Survive!*) are all hallmarks of exploitation film greatness, yet Cardona still hasn't received the recognition he is due.

It can't be the subject matter. Rene Cardona Jr. has a penchant for disaster movies. The more disastrous the better, and if Hollywood happened to make a large budget version of the story previously, then that's just fine. Unfortunately, Cardona is a big-scale tragedy film-maker on a single-location romantic comedy starring Carrot-Top budget. This never stopped the Latin King of Disaster (God, I hope that name sticks) in his never-ending quest for celluloid greatness though. His films, although many have never been released in North America, run the gamut of terror and tragedy. *Guyana: Crime of the Century* detailed the nefarious dealings of the Reverend Jim Jones and the mass suicide of the cult members. This feel-good tale of the year came out under the discerning eye of Cardona. *Guyana*, even though filmed in the usual micro-budget Cardona style, was actually picked up by Universal for release in the United States. One would think that Cardona's star was on the rise until, of course, Universal re-cut the film and added a narrator, effectively killing of Cardona's version of the piece.

Cardona followed up *Guyana* with a *Jaws*-like disaster film called *Tintorera* (*Tiger Shark*). It fails as a film on almost any cinematic level, but the tried and true method for Cardona's filmmaking is there. Take one part hugely successful storyline (in this case, *Jaws*), one part semi-recognizable American actor (*Tintorera* starred Priscilla Barnes of *Three's Company* fame), add stock footage, mix, and shake. Your final recipe should serve between 10 and 20 guests. This formula worked for Cardona and, unlike many exploitation filmmakers of the same time period, he actually made his living from the movies.

Cardona began his entertainment career at his father's side in 1949, acting in his first film, *Cartas Marcads*, in the role of a newsboy. Cardona Jr. appeared in many of his father's films and eventually began directing in 1964 with *El Raspado*. An accomplished writer as well, Cardona Jr. penned the screenplay for, arguably, his father's most famous film, *Night of the Bloody Apes* in 1968. Cardona also wrote many of his own films including *Cyclone, Tintorera* and *Evil Birds* (a Hitchcockian suspense thriller). It stands to reason that, at the very least, fans of genre films and exploitation masterpieces would be familiar with Rene Cardona Jr. This simply isn't the case.

This brings us to the reason we are here. *Cyclone.* A Rene Cardona, Jr. epic of the highest magnitude, this film has everything that made Cardona what he is today. A disaster, barely recognizable American actors (including Arthur Kennedy as a kindly priest and Lionel Stander, the gruff butler of *Hart to Hart* fame), gore, and a penchant for long spans of time where nothing happens makes *Cyclone* the perfect Cardona Starter Film for budding exploitation film enthusiasts. Walk with us, if you will, through the mind of Cardona. A freak ocean cyclone is about to hit a small Caribbean island. This disastrous storm (which ends a half hour into the film, oddly enough) takes down multiple boats, a plane and people on shore.

The focus of our story, though, is on a tour boat. Much like a B-movie version of *Gilligan's Island*, each of the passengers is a gross stereotype. You have the rich woman (international sexpot Carroll Baker), complete with dog, a pregnant woman and husband, a handsome boat captain (and young First Mate with which he exchanges serious homo-erotic glances at inopportune moments), and the rest. During the "largest storm in recorded history," the boat survives and, along the way, picks up the stranded passengers of a downed airplane and fishing boat. Prophetically, one of the characters sums up the plight of the storm survivors with one finely crafted line of dialogue. He states, "Our only hope is that they find us before it's too late." Well said, Bible-thumping crusty fisherman, well said.

Meanwhile, back on shore, we find out it isn't logical to keep looking for survivors. It seems the crack police force on Generic Island is pretty well suited to just not doing anything. All the bad news to the families of the dead is delivered under crystal blue skies. On the mainland, the threat has certainly passed.

On the boat, things have gone from bad to worse. Days afloat have reduced the water supply (from the melted ice in a cooler) to nothing. Food is scarce. This is a Cardona film, so thoughts naturally turn to cannibalism. You can see where this is going.

Cyclone, although not the greatest film in the world, is a very important part of both Mexican and worldwide exploitation film history. Cardona Jr. is often overshadowed by the image of his father, Cardona Sr., and the Lucha films that Sr. was notorious for. It is high time that Rene Cardona Jr., The Latin King of Exploitation, finally gets the recognition he deserves. Maybe deserves isn't the right word. Cardona worked his entire life to entertain the audiences that came to see his sometimes awful films. Undaunted, Cardona pressed on directing his last film in 2000. Cardona died on February 5, 2003, in Mexico City from cancer. Cardona, Jr. is survived by a son, Rene Cardona III, also a film director, who is carrying on the fine family tradition of Exploitive Filmmaking.

The Dead Next Door (1989)
by Andrew J. Rausch

Pop quiz: Name the early 1980s independent cult film that involved Sam Raimi (billed as "The Master Cylinder"), Bruce Campbell, and Scott Spiegel, in which the dead return to wreak havoc upon the living. Anyone who answered *The Evil Dead* or *Evil Dead 2* must now go directly to jail. Do not pass GO, do not collect $200. If you answered The Dead Next Door, give yourself a hearty pat on the back.

Yes, Sam Raimi, Bruce Campbell, and Scott Spiegel were all involved with the first two films in the *Evil Dead* trilogy and, indeed, they're both early 1980s independent cult flicks in which the dead return to wreak unholy havoc upon the living. The trick is that Raimi was never billed as "The Master Cylinder" on any of the *Evil Dead* films. Yeah, sue me.

I only recently stumbled upon *The Dead Next Door* courtesy of the Internet. A large number of web sites are dedicated to this lost gem. Upon discovery, my curiosity was piqued and I set out to find this film. Once I obtained a copy and sat down to view it for the first time, I was surprised at how effective the film was. As a low-budget zombie tale, it serves as a natural successor to films such as the *Evil Dead* trilogy and George Romero's *Night of the Living Dead*.

While *Night of the Living Dead* can be viewed as a cautionary tale of cold war nuclear paranoia and the *Evil Dead* films were used to showcase Raimi's extraordinary camera work, *The Dead Next Door* simply is what it is: "A movie for fanboys, directed by a fanboy" to paraphrase director J.R. Bookwalter. At times, the film seems cheesy and the production values sometimes appear lower than they are but that's not necessarily a bad thing. *The Dead Next Door* never takes itself too seriously. While watching the film, one can almost sense that Bookwalter wanted that camp feeling associated with classic B-movies.

In keeping with Bookwalter's genre fanboy demographic, *The Dead Next Door* contains a vast number of references to other zombie films. In the opening scene, a zombie stops by a video store to check out a VHS copy of Romero's *Dawn of the Dead*, and, presumably, to feast on the video clerk, as well. In a nod to his own genre heroes, Bookwalter laces the film with characters named after horror writers and filmmakers, such as (Sam) Raimi, (Stephen) King, (Tom) Savini, and (John) Carpenter.

While there is a definite satiric atmosphere present in *The Dead Next Door*, the level of cinematic brilliance Bookwalter often achieves is remarkable. Despite a low budget, Bookwalter managed to pull off a few incredible feats and, in the process, upped the ante for all zombie films to come. Born of raw genius or sheer madness, Bookwalter aspired for his zombies to achieve levels greater than their higher-budget predecessors. Where *Return of the Living Dead* implied that the living corpses might one day take over the nation, Bookwalter's zombies do it right before your eyes! Hell, they climb over the fence and on to the White House lawn!

Not allowing himself the credit he so rightly deserves, Bookwalter chalks his ambition up to naïveté, saying he didn't know what he was doing. Had he actually taken the time to consider it, he probably wouldn't have done some of the outrageous things he did. Naive or not, Bookwalter obviously has a keen cinematic sensibility.

The story behind Bookwalter and *The Dead Next Door* began in the mid-80s. With hopes of becoming a filmmaker, Bookwalter attended the Art Institute of Pittsburgh. Upon arrival, he envisioned working with the likes of locals George Romero and Tom Savini. Yet, the closest he came to this was a stint as a zombie extra on the *Day of the Dead* set. To make things worse, the Art Institute of Pittsburgh didn't teach much in the way of film classes. Dejected, Bookwalter dropped out in the middle of his sophomore year. In a search for inspiration, he pulled out a dusty stack of old Fangoria magazines. While leafing through them, he came to an article about Detroit filmmaker Sam Raimi's *The Evil Dead*. Realizing that Detroit is only a few hours from his hometown of Akron, Ohio, he called

Raimi's production company, Renaissance Pictures, in search of work as a production assistant.

After Raimi agreed to look at Bookwalter's work, the aspiring filmmaker drove like a maniac, heading for Detroit city limits. Upon showing Sam Raimi and Bruce Campbell his roughly made Super-8 films, the impressed Raimi made a nearly off-handed comment that he would consider funding a feature length project by Bookwalter. Sitting down behind a ratty old typewriter upon his return to Akron, Bookwalter began hammering out a screenplay that he finished in a week. "I think Bruce thought Sam was nuts for helping this kid no one really knew much about," Bookwalter remembers.

Campbell remembers things much the same way, "Yeah, I thought Sam was basically nuts. But, since before the first *Evil Dead* film, we all had a morbid fascination about whether or not a feature film really could be done in the Super-8 format. Sam decided to put his money where his mouth was."

Initially Bookwalter planned to shoot the entire thing on a budget of $8,000. "I don't know what I thought I could do with $8,000 and a video camera, but I was willing to try," Bookwalter reflects, laughing. Eventually, they decided to shoot *The Dead Next Door* on Super-8 and the budget soared to $125,000, an amount almost unheard of for such a grass roots-style film. "If nothing else, I just wanted to go out and try something bigger. I always bite off more than I can chew, I think. Things like the zombies on the White House fence and the aerial shots were certainly Spielbergian influences."

Bookwalter and crew applied for a permit, but were told that zombies absolutely could not be placed anywhere on the White House lawn or on the fence. Fully utilizing some big brass cojones, Bookwalter and crew shot the zombies on the White House fence without permits. They managed to get about one shot before Secret Service agents surrounded them. "We got totally busted," Bookwalter says, giggling like a schoolboy. "We passed it off like we were students and they let us go. Unfortunately there were some scratches on that footage, but that stuff is priceless."

Scott Spiegel, who wrote *Evil Dead 2*, agreed to appear in the film as a favor to Raimi. Spiegel would later appear in other Bookwalter-directed films, such as *Robot Ninja*. "J.R. knows what he wants," Spiegel says. "He shoots fast and you'd better know your lines.

No screwing around. But he's not a tyrant. He's very easy to deal with and open to all kinds of ideas."

Because of occasional budget problems, the shoot lasted four years. After shooting was finished came the task of correcting the film's unsalvageable sound. Transferring the tracks from their original Super-8 would cost a lot more than anyone wanted to spend at this point and would have caused the budget to balloon even more. Because of Bruce Campbell's previous sound engineering work at Renaissance Pictures, Raimi suggested that Campbell be in charge of correcting the sound problems. Once Campbell came on board, they decided to overdub all of the voices in the film. Campbell, Spiegel, and Bookwalter provided most of the characters' voices in the film.

"I was appointed to be the guy who would help supervise every shred of sound put to J.R.'s film," Campbell explains. "It had no useable production sounds whatsoever, so I took the approach that it might as well have been an Italian film and that we were just doing the English version. So, I rounded up a pile of actor friends and we all supplied the voices. It was a hoot, really."

This dubbing only further adds to the unique camp of *The Dead Next Door*, giving it the feel of a Lucio Fulci or Dario Argento film. In fact, the technical ineptness of *The Dead Next Door* serves to increase its stature by associating it with Italian horror as many hardcore horror junkies have come to believe that Italian horror films are superior to their U.S. counterparts.

According to Bookwalter, he and Campbell had daily disagreements regarding various aspects of the sound. "Bruce and I would be sitting there, practically having a screaming match—it would be that I wanted the music louder or he wanted the effects louder. We'd be fighting about something, then ten seconds later he'd crack some joke, and I'd be laughing so hard that I'd forgot all about it. He has this completely charming and disarming way of cutting through the BS. We'd split the difference and compromise, which is, of course, what this whole business is about. He had his marching orders from Sam (whatever those were at the time as far as what they wanted to get out of this movie and what they wanted to do with the sound), and I had my own ideas."

"Well, it was all about sensibilities," Campbell recalls. "I can't help but insist on certain procedures that I had become familiar with, regarding looping, foley and mixing philosophies. J.R. was just a filmmaker who was trying to get his flick made and I could never fault him for that. To my recollection, we got on all right, although I'm sure I came across as Sam's thug, sent in to oversee his world. Eventually, I did get Sam to cough up far more for sound than he had ever intended."

As visions of John Carpenter danced in his head, Bookwalter suggested that he score the film himself. Campbell agreed that it would be acceptable and quite a bit cheaper than paying someone else to compose music for the film. Looking back, Bookwalter calls his desire to score the film himself "an asinine idea that, if I were to do it over again, I would never have done!"

Eventually the film was completed and it slowly began to gain a cult following. "I've done random web searches on my name or *The Dead Next Door* and I'm always amazed when all this stuff comes up and you see all these fan pages," Bookwalter says. "They have audio clips and video clips, all these pictures and stuff that people have put up for *The Dead Next Door*... You start to realize that there are really people out there who are watching and becoming affected by this stuff."

Over the past few years, rumors have circulated that *The Dead Next Door* was actually directed by Sam Raimi. A foreign distributor actually went so far as to change the film's title to the unwieldy Sam Raimi Presents *The Dead Next Door: Another Evil Dead*. When I began working on this story for *Cashiers du Cinemart*, I asked one well-known genre director for his thoughts on *The Dead Next Door* and he went on to tell me that he believed Raimi actually made the film.

"Yes, I think it's pretty funny how misinformation spreads," Bookwalter says. "Then again, I've never really done anything to stop it. The few times I've seen people mention that Sam directed it; I just laughed and moved on. There are fifty cast and crew people and tons more who were peripherally involved that would also disagree after four long years of work!"

Dollman (1991)
by Brad Paulson

Ah, Full Moon. I remember the day when I used to see that logo roll up the screen and I would know I was in for a good movie. Well, most of the time anyway. This was also a time when Albert Pyun used to make good movies on a regular basis. For a while, I was even a Full Moon fan club member.

Coming off the success of *Cyborg* (which is another one of my favorite trash cinema classics), Pyun essentially created a stylized look that Asylum attempted to rip off years later. However, when Full Moon did it (or Albert Pyun I should say), it actually looked like a sci-fi movie. When Asylum did it, they just made it look like a crappy orange or green filter was attached to the lens. Now they follow suit with the Syfy Channel and make everything look like one of their movies.

Dollman features the man, the myth, the legend: Tim Thomerson. He's been one of my favorite actors since the glory days of Full Moon and someone I also had the good fortune to meet when I first moved to L.A.

It was at a Hollywood Sci-Fi/Horror convention in the Roosevelt Hotel that I first met Thomerson and gave him a script I had written. He gladly took it, but I didn't hear from him after that because there was no money attached. It wasn't until years after I had moved to the land of broken halos that I discovered it took a lot more to get a movie made than just putting a script in the hands of an actor. I wasn't upset or even disillusioned. It's not as if I expected Jack Deth (my favorite of Thomerson's movie character names) to work for free.

Six months or so after the convention, I landed a temp job over at the talent agency Innovative Artists in Santa Monica. I sighted more than a few celebrities in my time there. One day I was even in the elevator with Michael Richards from *Seinfeld* (before he dropped the n-bomb and the proverbial scat hit the fan). Even though I'm a big fan of his Stanley Spadowski character in the Weird Al classic *UHF*, it was Thomerson who I really wanted to fanboy up to.

When I discovered Innovative repped him, I was thrilled. Ecstatic. Amazed beyond belief. To a guy like me, at that time in my life, meeting the star of *Trancers*, *Dollman*, and *Dollman vs. Demonic Toys* (among many other greats) was far more important than meeting someone like Tom Cruise.

One day when I was in the mailroom making photocopies of headshots, I picked up Thomerson's and told my coworkers how great he is. As it turns out, the assistant to Thomerson's agent overheard my nerd-driven speech and said, "You really like Tim Thomerson, don't you?"

"Absolutely. He's only about the finest movie star who ever lived."

"Uh, yeah. Of course," he responded without nearly any of the enthusiasm I had just shown. And although he didn't exactly match my level of nerd praise for the great Tim Thomerson, he did find my relentless toadying of his boss's client humorous.

"You know he's coming in tomorrow, right?"

"Really?" I asked. I was not expecting to hear this.

"If you want, I can have him drop by your desk and say hi."

"Dude, that would be fucking awesome!" (or something of that nature) was my reply.

He had a goofy grin on his face as he walked off. I probably gave him material to make fun of me for the rest the year on just that day alone.

The morning rolled around and it felt like Christmas knowing that Tim Thomerson was going to show up at the office. I was excited, but I was also nervous. I was afraid I was going to say and/or do something stupid; two things that have and still have a good chance of happening with me.

Now Tim couldn't exactly drop by my desk because I didn't have one. I was known as what they call a floater. This means I would go from the mailroom to cover an assistant's desk when one of them didn't show up for the day. So, I had to make sure I was hanging out by a desk and waiting for Tim to show up.

Even though noise was everywhere, it may as well have been silent because I heard nothing but the sound of my own voice (and there were a lot of very vocal people in that place). And then it happened: the unmistakable voice of Jack Deth echoed down the hallway:

"All right, where's this kid who's a big fan of mine? I want to talk to this guy!"

Thomerson showed up and bullshitted with me for about a half hour. He regaled me with stories of his adventures that were unsuitable for all audiences. He was a charismatic, fantastic storyteller. I was walking on clouds for the rest of week (even though I realized Thomerson would now probably never do my movie because he knew that I was just a low-budget mailroom lackey). The charisma Thomerson showed in our meeting transcends itself into his onscreen performances. *Dollman* is no exception.

Thomerson's entrance in the film is basically a nod to Sylvester Stallone's in *Cobra* (which was a nod to Clint Eastwood's in *Dirty Harry*). Another nod to *Dirty Harry* is the gun Thomerson's character lugs around: a Kruger blaster, the most powerful handgun in the universe (as a fat kid lets us know at a very humorous moment in the film). Thomerson's Brick Bardo character in *Dollman* is essentially an amalgamation of these iconic movie cops. Looking like a bad ass, wearing sunglasses and cracking wise, Bardo goes into the opening hostage situation and does his laundry, while a Keith Richards-esque bad guy holds several fat ladies and kids hostage.

Bardo's confrontation with the criminal ends in a humorous climax and even though he is victorious, his superiors still protest that he's a loose cannon. Things only get worse for Bardo as he's framed for a massive crime and ambushed by a flying head belonging to a man named Sprug. He's a little upset that Bardo took every body part away from him except for the head. We soon learn this was done out of revenge for what Sprug did to Bardo's family.

Then, after a chase where Thomerson goes after the flying head in his own spaceship (who knows how he'd even get that thing to fly?), Bardo's and Sprug's ships crash and they land somewhere even more horrifying than the outer reaches of space: the South Bronx.

Upon landing, Bardo discovers that not only is he in a shitty barrio, but here on planet Earth he's only thirteen inches tall, a perfect height for engaging in fisticuffs with other action figures, but to dwarves, he's shoe fodder. Fortunately for Bardo, he's got his Kruger blaster and it proves deadly even to the giant-sized human scum he's up against. His nemesis Sprug is also toy sized. That makes things a little easier for Bardo, but blasting his way out of this shitty neighborhood proves to be no walk in the park. Especially when the main giant villain is played by Jackie Earle Haley of *Breaking Away, A Nightmare on Elm Street,* and *Watchmen* fame. And although Haley was amazing in *Watchmen,* every time his name is brought up I always think of *Dollman.*

Bardo ends up befriending and forming an alliance with a local woman named Maria to battle Haley and Sprug and make his way back home.

I must admit I have a personal bias for this film because I'm not only a Thomerson fan but also a dwarf lover. In *Dollman,* one of my favorite actors became even smaller than a dwarf, which is even more awesome.

Dollman is a fun movie with a sense of humor that includes Thomerson shooting a cockroach with his Kruger blaster, a space chase with a flying head, a cigarette-smoking, half-exploded thug, and a criminal crushed by fat women (among many other wonderful things).

Equinox (1970)
by E.D. Tucker

In 1965, a group of friends and special effects enthusiasts who were all children of the *Famous Monsters of Filmland* generation, decided to make a monster movie of their very own. Dennis Muren, Mark McGee, Jim Danforth, and Dave Allen were all just budding talents at the time but they were destined for greatness that would inspire subsequent generations. With the help of unpaid friends, family, and peers with the same desire to make a movie, they completed a fun little tale of black magic called *The Equinox...A Journey into the Supernatural*.

The basic plot concerns four college students on a double date who decide to visit one of their professors at his remote cabin. What they didn't count on was that the professor had located an ancient text, presumably the Necronomicon, and opened a gateway to another dimension. After his cabin is trashed and the professor is killed, the book ends up in the hands of a crazy hermit who, in turn, passes it off to the students, proving that maybe he isn't so crazy after all. For the remainder of the film, the quartet is assaulted by all manner of evil creatures until the final survivor ends up in a mental institution with a curse on his head.

This version of *Equinox* was filled with ambitious and often impressive special effects, notable for both their creativity and variety. These included a cool ape monster, a not so jolly blue giant, and a flying horned demon. Unfortunately, the story lacked structure, most of the dialog had to be re-recorded, and the running time was short. The finished product lacked professional polish and it failed to interest distributors. It would languish on Dennis Muren's shelf for several years until producer Jack H. Harris discovered it.

Harris, best known for pitting young Steve McQueen against *The Blob* in 1958, knew an exploitable movie when he saw one. He also recognized *Equinox* as the collection of effects pieces it was and realized that the connecting story would require shoring up. He contacted Jack Woods, a talented editor, for help in expanding the central plot and lengthening the running time. Woods not only concocted a revised story, but also directed the new footage and starred as a newly added villain.

In the new story, the original plot is retained up to the point where the group receives the book. They then run afoul of a satanic park ranger portrayed, surprisingly well, by Jack Woods. In the new version, the ranger spends his time trying to retrieve the book, and the monsters from the salvaged effects footage are shown to be summoned by him to do his bidding. When he's not busy controlling his creatures, the strange ranger also tries to possess the teens and even makes a really bizarre rape attempt on one of the young ladies.

Some additional padding was also filmed of the group having a picnic lunch and trying to open the book. A subplot was added about mystical objects protecting them and they are shown making talismans out of twigs and string. A few of the special effects scenes were enhanced or re-edited to improve the presentation and better integrate them with the new scenes. A lengthy dialogue piece was lost at the end to incorporate the ranger character transforming into the final demon but most viewers never missed the exposition or questioned the plot holes.

In the end, very little footage from the non-effect sequences of the original version of *Equinox* was retained. Fortunately all four of the principal actors were able to return for the new shoot, so continuity loss was kept to a minimum. Since the original film was shot over the course of a year and the re-shoots were done almost five years later, you can see the hair lengths and styles change multiple times in the same scene! There was also only one set of the original wardrobe available so the actors had to be careful not to damage any of their clothes while climbing up cliffs and running from monsters.

Jack Harris shortened the film's title to simply *Equinox*, and it was finally released to theaters in 1970. It played for several years, first in stand-alone billings and then on the bottom half of double features with other horror movies, including the Jacksonville,

Florida-lensed *ZAAT*. After that, the PG-rated tale of demons, satanic cults, and attempted rape made the kiddie matinee circuit where I first saw it on the big screen as part of a children's summer movie series! Needless to say, we howled like the uncivilized monkeys we were during the rape scene where Jack Woods slobbers all over poor Barbara Hewitt.

Equinox made a big impression on me as a kid and I would not get to see it again until many years later when it was released on home video. By the time I was reunited with the film, Dennis Muren had already graduated to a little film called *Star Wars* and continues to work on Hollywood blockbusters to this day. His partners in crime did not fair quite as well but all went on to pay the bills by working steadily in film production. Jim Danforth and Dave Allen are both heralded as successors to the special effects legacy pioneered by Willis O'Brian and honed to perfection by Ray Harryhausen. Of the actors, only Frank Bonner continued after this film but he is best remembered for his stint on *WKRP in Cincinnati* as Herb Tarlek.

If the plot of *Equinox* sounds vaguely familiar, that's because it bears a striking similarity to the cult classic *Evil Dead* that was made a little over a decade later. The group of college friends, the professor discovering the book and awaking evil forces, and even some of the drawings used to illustrate the Necronomicon are all right out of the first part of *Equinox*. The second half of *Equinox* is an homage to the science fiction movies of the 1950s where director Sam Rami chose to take *Evil Dead* into the realm of extreme violence laced with slapstick comedy, but it's hard to imagine him not having seen *Equinox* at some earlier point in his life.

For anyone who has never seen this little independent oddity or those that need an excuse to revisit it, Criterion has released an excellent two DVD set for the film. The first disc contains both versions of the movie so that fans can finally compare the young filmmakers' original vision to the more theatrically viable edition. The second disc is loaded with extras related to the film and also to the careers of some of its participants. This serves as an excellent reminder of the creative talents that joined forces on this supernatural labor of love.

Evil Bong (2006)
by Albert Sessoms

Before I give my thoughts on the film, I have to relate my first experience with *Evil Bong*. I am at my buddy's house and we are just sitting around watching *Breaking Bad*. I look over and see a DVD lying by its lonesome. *Evil Bong 1/Evil Bong 2*. Walt and Jesse can wait. Having always been a huge fan of the stoner movie sub-culture, I'm immediately intrigued by the strange and wonderful potential of this as-yet-unseen piece of cinema history. I inquired of my friend as to how this exciting film ever came to be in his possession.

He only gave me a funny look and turned his attention back to watching Gus Fring pontificate and Hector Salamenca ring his incessant bell. I invited him to share with me the details of the mythology in which the story was constructed. How is the Bong evil? What kind of evil is it? Lawful, neutral, or chaotic? Does it attack with little bong hands and a little bong knife or does it handle its depraved acts in a more sinister manner? My friend quickly pauses the DVR, grabs the DVD, and throws it at me. I give my thanks to him and assure him that I will return it soon. He replies, "You can have it. It's dumb. I don't want it anymore. Just shut up, already!"

So with that fanfare and without further ado, my thoughts on this forgotten piece of trash cinema...

First off, you can't have a serious discussion about the intellectual and artistic merits of this film without delving into the transitions haphazardly placed in between every fourth scene or so. It's like *Home Improvement*/original *Batman* television style as weed leaves spin across the screen, taking us from one scene to the next. Now,

I'm not sure if this was maybe a problem in the editing department where the director didn't have the shots the editor needed to make smooth scene transitions, or if this was a conscious choice by the screenwriter, but whoever was responsible needs to be fired. Not just fired though, they need to make sure this guy is not allowed to make any creative decisions in the future. I mean *nothing*. Like make him in charge of getting coffee, but don't forget to write down exactly what you want in it, or he is bound to fuck it up. Badly.

The cheesy music and acting make the movie feel like a porno film is going to break out at any moment. I mean, the most compelling thespian in the whole thing was the voice actor for the bong. Seriously. The bong calls one of the vapid chicks we meet a bitch, and I had a hard time finding a flaw in the bong's logic. I found myself rooting for the bong to murder everyone else in the cast with the worst actors (a.k.a everyone) hopefully dying quicker than the others (a.k.a the bong). The rest of the ensemble go through much of the film lacking any real emotion or fluctuations beyond deadpan, and when they do you will wish they hadn't even made the attempt at an actual human emotion.

Probably the strangest moment (of many; Sharkboob anyone?) was in the sequence where the bong (who looks amazingly similar to a certain Doctor Who villain) pulls in her first victim. A stripper approaches our victim with a couple of skulls built into her brassiere. She proceeds to let the skulls chomp away at our victim's face. Then a small looking something (that is obviously a puppet or moppet or whatever) pops up into view and starts to jerk off as the victim's blood sprays everywhere. Tres bizzaro, little dude.

Thankfully, Tommy Chong shows up a little more than halfway in to save this movie from utter wretchedness. He is the previous owner of the bong and he has come to destroy it once and for all. As he goes to work the last drug-free kid decides to hit the bong so he is able to enter his evil realm. But get this, he goes to save a girl he has met twice and doesn't think twice about his friends/roommates that are going to be possibly trapped inside the evil bong forever. Finally the straight edge kid and his girl take some anti-weed medication and are able to escape the clutches of the evil bong and her marijuana lair.

As Chong is finally successful in taking out the resourceful bong, we are left with the line that is truly representative of the entire film itself as Chong utters the immortal words, "Put this in your pipe, you evil bitch!" A microcosm of trash cinema at its finest. The rest of the people taken by the bong are returned to the regular world and even the dead roommates are returned to life. (In a good, non-zombie/*Pet Sematary* way). Of course they set up for a sequel, *Evil Bong II: King Bong*. After doing a search on Google I found that there is actually a newly-made third installment, *Evil Bong III: The Wrath of Bong*. So stay tuned, readers—trash cinema is alive and well, and we have only scratched the surface!

Evil Ever After (2006)
by Andrew J. Rausch

Let's just get this straight right from the get-go: writers/directors Brad Paulson and Chris Watson are a couple of sick puppies. And their movie *Evil Ever After?* Yeah, it's some sick shit, too. It's the kind of oddity that cinematic nightmares and gory cult movie dreams are made of.

Due to piss-poor "international" distribution from CryptKeeper Entertainment, this little gem, produced for less than $10,000, is languishing away in the Land of Forgotten Films right now. And that's a shame, because this little chiller is quite brilliant in a sort of mentally deranged way. It deserves to be seen so that it can sicken and disturb audiences in a way that only a balls-to-the-wall, no-holds-barred movie made by a couple of sick bastards like Paulson and Watson can.

"I was fairly uncomfortable with the piece but interested in working on the motion picture because I liked the filmmakers and the cast," explains actor Ford Austin. "In the end, I committed fully to the debaucherously low behavior of my character, and I felt proud about the end result."

So what exactly is so bad, er, good, about this movie? No one's saying this is a *good* movie (at least not by accepted Hollywood standards)—only that it is an extremely effective and repulsive one that may cause audiences to vomit on their laps and then also squirm uncomfortably in their seats for a ridiculously inordinate measure of time. Remember that still-shocking, extended rape scene from the original *I Spit on Your Grave?* That, my friends, is nothing compared to what *Evil Ever After* has in store for its viewers. This film's rape scene, in which Harvey (Austin) anally rapes Bernie Grisso

(Randal Malone), takes the cake. It is as disturbing and discomforting as anything ever committed to film, and it feels like it goes on for something like ten to twenty minutes. This scene, in all its vulgar, cringe-inducing glory, makes the rape scene from *I Spit on Your Grave* look like something out of a Disney flick. It also feels very real, as if we're watching a real-life rape unfold before our eyes.

There is a good reason for this, explains actor Ford Austin. "The rape scene was real. We never intended for the scene to actually happen like that. Once Randal Malone, Aaron Burke, and I were in the scene, the moment completely took us over and we couldn't stop. I heard years later, from Randal Malone, that he has been dealing with the effects from that evening ever since."

Remember how that foot-slicing scene from Takashi Miike's *Audition* made you squirm? Remember how disoriented *Last House on the Left* made you feel the first time you watched it? Again, as strange as it may sound, these experiences are nothing compared to the sheer discomfort you will feel watching this little curiosity.

"Chris and I were trying to accomplish the craziest drive-in style movie we could given the extremely low budget we had," Paulson recalls. "We looked at movies to use as a template we could put a twist on, and *I Spit on Your Grave* kept coming up. It's a powerful movie. It disturbs me every time I see it. Cross it with Larry Clark's *Bully*, and we came up with *Evil Ever After*. Honestly, I don't know what we were thinking. We were young, had an opportunity, and wanted to do something people with brains that worked wouldn't even think about releasing in a theater."

There are a handful of fine performances in *Evil Ever After*, from the likes of Brinke Stevens, Joe Bob Briggs, and Joe Estevez, but future *Dahmer vs. Gacy* leads Austin and Malone steal the show here. Malone gives a very wrenching, extremely honest performance as Grisso, a cross-dressing cannibalistic psychopath wielding a samurai sword and bent on bloody revenge. And Austin? Well, Austin is Austin, which is always a good thing. Here he gives his most deliciously evil performance since his appearance in director Watson's otherwise forgettable *Slaughter Party*.

"The filming of the rape scene was bizarre to say the least," Paulson explains. "In fact, the filming of the entire movie was surreal. It was like orchestrating a giant circus act. Originally the goal was to make the scene longer than the one in *I Spit on Your Grave*, but I think it ended up around ten minutes... I actually tried to scale the scene back, but Randal wanted it to be authentic and disturbing. We got a bunch of beer so everyone could relax. Shit got weird fast. We crammed 10 pages of dialogue into a few hours of shooting. I think Ford only had about a tenth of it memorized when we started, but I'll be damned if he didn't learn it fast and commit himself to the part 100 percent. Things escalated to a frenzy pitch. Once that train got rolling, the shit didn't stop for anyone."

Chris Watson explains, "When the movie was first screened in Los Angeles, it was broken into two parts. It stopped after the rape scene and there was a break. The lights came up and it had people talking and numerous looks of disgust. It was great. That scene gets brought up a lot."

Former TV monster movie host Joe Bob Briggs (a.k.a. John Bloom) appears as an alcoholic father who regularly molests his daughter. "Mighty" Mike Murga plays a caged, rabid, angry dwarf who feeds on human flesh. Julie and Lizzy Strain turn up as a couple of topless strippers, giving co-director Watson the strangest, most unappealing lap dance of all time. (One of them actually does the "robot" dance, which is about as sexually alluring as a punch in the face.) This movie has penis mutilations, disembowelment, the aforementioned extended anal rape scene, cannibalism, gore, gore, and more gore, incest, face-pissing, you name it... It feels like Paulson and Watson just sat down and made a list of everything awful (and, to their credit, memorable) they could think of to shoehorn into *Evil Ever After*, and in no way am I suggesting that's a bad thing.

"I don't see any reason to make a micro movie if people are going to forget it a week later," Watson says. "I wanted to see something akin to a vile circus."

"No matter how many things I would have done differently were I to get the chance to do it again," Paulson says, "I got to make a movie with Joe Bob Briggs, Brinke Stevens, Joe Estevez, Julie Strain, Felissa Rose, and power dwarf Mighty Mike Murga, and I'll be damned if that isn't awesome in and of itself. Why make a movie with Tom Cruise when you can use a real dwarf?"

Evil Ever After is that rarest of movies that will affect its viewers long after they've hit the "stop" button on their DVD players (which, for some, is likely to come long before the film's conclusion). It's a dirty, depraved little ditty that will make you want to take a long hot shower after you've finished watching it.

Faster, Pussycat! Kill! Kill! (1965)
by Stephen Spignesi

1. On Watching the Beginning of *Faster, Pussycat! Kill! Kill!*

Depending on who you listen to, Russ Meyer is either a great talent or a talentless hack.

Roger Ebert liked *Faster, Pussycat! Kill! Kill!* John Waters called it the greatest movie ever made. Other critics call it the worst movie ever made. As of this writing (ten minutes into the movie), I am in the latter camp. (I had never seen the whole flick until asked to write about it.)

I admit up front that I am not a fan of camp. I am also not a fan of comic book movies or animation. (I'm probably the only Tarantino fan who did not like the "Origin of O-Ren" anime sequence in *Kill Bill!* And I'm probably the only Woody Allen fan who wasn't ensorcelled by the animated sequence in *Annie Hall*.)

Yes, I do know that *Faster, Pussycat! Kill! Kill!* is not animated. And this is where the camp comes in. The movie is so over the top, it could have been animated and, for its purposes, would have worked just as well.

We get a sense of what we're in for with the stentorian opening narration, set against old sci-fi-looking wavy lines that suggest...I have no idea what they suggest:

Ladies and gentlemen, welcome to violence, the word and the act. While violence cloaks itself in a plethora of disguises, its favorite mantle still remains...sex. Violence devours all it touches, its voracious appetite rarely fulfilled. Yet violence doesn't only destroy, it creates and molds as well. Let's examine closely then this dangerously evil creation, this new breed encased and contained within the supple skin of woman. The softness is there, the unmistakable smell of female, the surface shiny and silken, the body yielding yet wanton. But a word of caution: handle with care and don't drop your guard. This rapacious new breed prowls both alone and in packs, operating at any level, any time, anywhere, and with anybody. Who are they? One might be your secretary, your doctor's receptionist...or a dancer in a go-go club!

This repugnantly misogynistic tirade is followed by scenes of Go-Go dancers gyrating pseudo-sexily while being shrieked at by a repulsive, middle-aged mouth-breather; one of those brutes who make all men look bad. He bellows insanely, "Let's go!" over and over at the dancers with what is probably supposed to be a look of uncontrollable lust on his face, but which is actually serial-killer-esque, puke-worthy, pinhead-ish grotesqueness. This scene is hideous beyond belief.

So, let's recap:

So far, the characters are idiots.

So far, the dialogue is abominable.

So far, the acting is a Master Class in Bad Acting.

But this is supposed to be a *fun* movie, a guilty pleasure, and an exploitation classic, right?

This is the first time I've seen it, and I wouldn't have watched past the first ten minutes or so had I not had to watch it for this writing assignment.

So I'll take one for the team and my friend Coach Andy and see what the rest of *Faster, Pussycat! Kill! Kill!* has to offer.

2. After The Bostweeds Conclude their 1'10" *Pussycat* Theme and "The End" Is Onscreen

So (spoiler alert), the non-vegetable brother and the pretty, young kidnap victim live, and drive off into the desert dirt.

Three Go-Go dancers named Varla, Rosie, and Billie, go joy-riding in sports cars in the desert, which apparently requires hysterical shrieking and laughing because they're driving fast. They come across a young couple. Varla, the leader, ends up killing the boy and they kidnap the girl. They then come upon an old man living with his two sons out in the desert and they decide to stick around long enough to scheme the old man out of his money (brilliantly hidden in the seat of his wheelchair. Mensa members these characters are not.). One of the sons is mentally challenged; the father is wheelchair-bound. After a modicum of sex and violence (and abominable, innuendo-laden dialogue), everyone ends up dead except the young kidnap victim and the normal brother. Cue The Bostweeds. (And speaking of the old man, there's a scene in which his son is pushing him across the desert in his wheelchair and it cannot help but remind *Breaking Bad* fans of Hector Salamanca in his wheelchair after his stroke. Is Vince Gilligan a Russ Meyer fan? The father also looks like and is dressed like Salamanca, so truth be told, all he needs is the bell!)

Faster, Pussycat! Kill! Kill! was the first Russ Meyer film I watched in its entirety, and I did, in fact, experience a CO—a Cleavage Overdose—after watching, and I needed to screen a few episodes of *Breaking Amish* to re-establish my psychosexual balance. (The white caps with the strings hanging down did the job.)

So, is there, as has been said, a lot to love about *Faster, Pussycat! Kill! Kill!?*

Yes and no. There is no doubting the misogyny and hypersexualizing of females in the film. And I'm not crazy about the equation proffered in the opening narration: violence = sex = woman.

But maybe you're overthinking this, I overthought. To get a female perspective on this, I asked my cowriter Rachel Montgomery to watch the film and make some notes regarding her response to it.

Rachel is in her early twenties and just earned her Master's in English. She has studied gender roles and patriarchy in American society, and grew up with feminism being an accepted part of her life. She is an independent thinker.

So I was very curious as to how she'd respond to a 1965 exploitation flick in which women are reduced to big-boobed stereotypes who seem to exist solely to wreak violent havoc and have sex.

Well, surprisingly, Rachel liked it. And she wasn't offended by it. She thought it was fun, and she interpreted it as an over-the-top, popular culture response to early feminism. The sixties brought new sexual freedoms, Rachel said, and new venues for assertion by women, and she believes that exploitation films like *Faster,*

Pussycat! were a (male) response to changing times and mores.

She actually saw the film as a *parody* of misogyny, rather than a manifestation or, heaven forefend, an endorsement of it. That interpretation speaks to the camp, excessive tone and cartoon-like sensibility of the film. The women are hyper-masculinized. They are overly aggressive, overly sexual, overly violent, and one could certainly analyze those traits and tropes as a response to feminism. *See what could happen if you let women have rights?!* the hysterical macho response could be.

This is a valid analysis and I don't think it's coincidental that of the four male characters in the film, only the softer, "feminine" character survives. The kidnap victim's boyfriend is murdered by Varla and, of the desert family, the male figures are "less than" men: the father is crippled, and the other son is mentally challenged. And then they are made dead by the Amazonian women. Since the very feminine Linda and the feminized brother are the only survivors, one of the themes could be that these new "women who want to be men" feminists are destined to die off. And, in a sense, the dead males represent the death of the Old Guard. To sexists, femininity (and by extension, feminism) has long been seen as needing to be tamed. And in *Faster, Pussycat! Kill! Kill!*, the metaphorical new liberated women of the sixties are not only tamed, they're eliminated.

So what is *Faster, Pussycat! Kill! Kill!*? Is it an anti-feminist screed? Is it a statement about the death of the patriarchal, macho male? Or is it a violent B-movie with over-the-top overacting; campy, sometimes awful dialogue; and a plethora of large breasts that certainly get their share of screen time?

I suspect that the answer to all those questions is "Yes."

Flash Gordon (1980)
by Mark Edlitz

If George Lucas had succeeded in his attempt to make a Flash Gordon movie, *Star Wars* might not have been made. Lucas was inspired by the 1936 black-and-white, 13-episode serial version of the movie and its two sequels, which starred the dashing Buster Crabbe and was based on Alex Raymond's comic strip hero. So after the success of *American Graffiti*, he set out to turn his childhood hero into a feature film. But when Lucas couldn't come to terms with King Features Syndicate, the original distributor of the strip, he channeled his passion for rocket ships and ray guns into creating his own far, far away galaxy. *Star Wars*, of course, turned out to be a massive hit and the rights to Flash Gordon remained ripe for the taking.

Dino De Laurentiis, one of the last of the great film moguls, thought that he had a blockbuster in the making when he optioned the rights to the perennially popular character, and he assembled an impressive team of filmmakers. He hired Mike Hodges, who directed the taut and much-praised thriller *Get Carter*, to helm the film. Lorenzo Semple, Jr., who wrote *Papillon*, starring Steve McQueen and Dustin Hoffman, and *Three Days of the Condor*, starring Robert Redford, was enlisted to pen the script. And two-time Oscar winner Danilo Donati, a frequent Federico Fellini collaborator, was tapped as the film's production designer, set designer and costume designer.

De Laurentiis believed that if he could capture even half the magic of *Star Wars*, his science fiction fantasy would rake in the cash. Surely his creative team could be entrusted to create a popular entertainment, if not an obvious *Star Wars* knockoff. De Laurentiis, who had worked with Semple on *King Kong*, thought that the screenwriter would handle *Flash Gordon* with the same melodramatic solemnity that he brought to *King Kong*. Instead, as he did while writing the TV series *Batman*, Semple treated the material as farce.

One could make a case that the outlandish plot calls for a humorous touch. Dr. Hans Zarkov (Topol) discovers that a sinister force is bent on destroying the Earth. In his effort to save the planet, Zarkov kidnaps Flash Gordon (Sam J. Jones) and Dale Arden (Melody Anderson) to assist him. The trio crash-lands Zarkov's space ship on Planet Mongo, where they are captured and held captive by the despot Ming the Merciless (Max von Sydow). After escaping the ruler's clutches Flash unites two warring tribes, falls in love, liberates the people of Mongo, defeats Ming and saves Earth.

Semple wrote some wonderful lines for the well-cast actors to play with. It takes a special kind of actor to deliver such delightfully over the top lines as "No one, but no one dies in the palace without a command from the Emperor." When Flash is battling Prince Barin (a pre-Bond Timothy Dalton) Dale encourages him to vanquish his opponent quickly, "Flash, I love you, but we only have fourteen hours to save the Earth!" As Ming, Von Sydow delivers many delicious speeches including, "Pathetic earthlings. Hurling your bodies out into the void, without the slightest inkling of who or what is out here. If you had known anything about the true nature of the universe, anything at all, you would've hidden from it in terror."

While the script is decidedly pulpy, it's no more absurd than much of the hyperbolic dialogue in *Star Wars*. Although the cast knew they were working on a larger than life canvas, neither they nor De Laurentiis initially thought they were entering the realm of camp. That all changed when the crew joined them for a screening of the dailies. Sam J. Jones recalled, "We played it straight, we couldn't have played it any other way. When the crew watched the rushes and were laughing hysterically, Dino said, 'Why are you laughing?' And then they discovered they had a comedy."

Unlike Lucas's lived-in *Star Wars* universe, everything in *Flash Gordon*, which was released in 1980, looks brand new and sumptuous. The Flash Gordon super fan and comic book artist Alex Ross told me, "This was definitely the effect of the disco era. Everything looks like you had just walked into Studio 54. This was a planet that was out of Andy Warhol's nightmares or dreams—whichever might be the case." In fact, Warhol was also big fan of the film. Film critic Pauline Kael, one of the few mainstream defenders of the film, called Flash Gordon a "[F]airy tale set in a discothèque in the clouds…The images are flooded with the primary colors of comic strips—blue and, especially, red at its most blazing…the colors [are] so ripely intense that they're near-psychedelic."

Though some criticize the voluptuous look of the film, Ross defends it, "I know that approach doesn't work for most people today. We have such a slender allowance for what you can allow science fiction [to] be today." While the bright vivid colors of the sets and costumes would be wholly out of place in Lucas' galaxy, the look of the film was true to Alex Raymond's original drawings. Ross added, "They didn't just make sets and costumes that fulfilled their own idiosyncrasies. They took the visual elements of the comics and turned them into physical approximations."

Unlike John Williams's timeless *Star Wars* score, Queen's pounding soundtrack inexorably links the movie to the Seventies. For his part, Ross thinks Queen's irrefutably stirring music is the pièce de résistance of the film. "When you're hearing that driving drumbeat leading up to the chorus of Flash it still captives arenas full of people—where they play it to this day. The music excites. It engages like someone just placed a certain button on the back of your head. The music is the final cherry on top of a Sundae that frankly De Laurentiis didn't intend to eat."

For what's ostensibly a family friendly film, there is a surprising amount of overt sexuality. In one scene Flash is stripped down and made to wear black leather underwear, and in another scene Ming's daughter, Princess Aura, rubs her hands all over Flash's near naked and (temporarily) dead body. Later in the film after Aura is tortured and whipped by another woman, one of Ming's henchmen observes, "I think she found it rather enjoyable." In addition to these scenes laced with sadomasochism there are references to incest, rape and necrophilia.

Ross observed, "*Star Wars* is completely sex abstinent. There is a complete androgyny in those films. In *Flash* there is subliminal sexuality. It's edgy and seditious. It's sexier and more sex defined than most straight films." For Hodges, inserting sexuality into the film was a calculated decision, "I hoped I'd be able to run two parallel films—one for children, the other for their parents. When I talked to American male friends who had been brought up on Flash Gordon they all said a lot of their sexual fantasies had come from it. I capitalized on that."

As a hero, Flash Gordon is cut from different cloth than Luke Skywalker who, over the course of three films, goes on a symbolic passage of self-discovery that Joseph Campbell termed the Hero's Journey. Ross told me, "The hero in Flash Gordon has arrived fully formed. He doesn't have to go through a metamorphosis or a change. He's not broken. He shows up in a world that is broken that has need of a hero to help it." Film critic Roger Ebert shared Ross's assessment when he wrote, "It's fun to see it done with energy and love and without the pseudo-meaningful apparatus of the Force and Trekkie Power."

Flash Gordon has so many disparate elements—the pulpy dialogue, the lavish sets, the rock music sound—that the film doesn't feel as if it's serving a unified vision. Whereas most movies require a cohesive style to work, Flash Gordon is enjoyable despite, and perhaps in part because, it's such a crazy quilt of different visions. Ross said, "I think there was a sense of chaos on set. You've got an Italian crew working in England with an English production. With an English director. With an American screenwriter. And a few American actors mixed in with English actors. [Along with the Swedish Von Sydow and a couple of Italian featured players.] The whole thing was a mess."

When the film was released, audiences weren't too sure what to make of this strange brew and, as a result, the box office results were middling; the domestic take was a little over $27 million. ($73 million when adjusted for inflation.) Audience response aside, the fact that such an eclectic big budget science fiction film was made is a fluke. Ross observes, "Normally you get one popular interpretation that leads to everything else. It's an amazing little point in history. *Flash* was made before things were so affected by the vision of George Lucas. Filmmakers were still experimenting with how to make a Sci-Fi film."

Flash Gordon is an action-packed, candy-colored space opera that can be a joy to behold. The key to enjoying the film is to appreciate and relish its eccentricities without judgment. As Ross laments,

"Nowadays you wouldn't make a film like *Flash Gordon*. It's an accident of sorts. Which is a shame."

Flesh Eating Mothers (1988)
by Allen Richards

What was your game-changer? What was it that opened your eyes to the notion that horror could be more than haunted houses, monsters, or dickheads chasing teenagers? That genre pieces could be socially relevant and deeply personal works of art that didn't merely entertain but also provoked interpretation, reflection, and, ultimately, introspection?

For me there were two works. Joe R. Lansdale's novella *The Drive-In* changed the way I viewed the printed word. For a teenager who grew up on Encyclopedia Brown and *Star Trek* novels, it was a revelation. I must have read it ten or twelve times before I hit twenty. Every chance I could I pimped it out. Two separate readings in 11th grade Speech & Drama (much to the annoyance of my teacher, Mrs. Wheeler), and then there was that dog-eared spare copy I forced on all my friends in college. Everyone admitted it was riot, but also that they couldn't see what it was that made it so special to me.

The same goes for my cinema game-changer—James Aviles Martin's *Flesh Eating Mothers*, the best Troma movie Troma never made. That video store poster I picked up from my local rental shop for fifty cents hung somewhere in my various houses and apartments until I was well into my thirties. The title alone was enough to intrigue anyone who saw it, and while all declared the movie "a hoot," none could understand the special place the movie had in my heart.

To hell with those people. If they don't get it, they don't get it. If the subtext, satire, and skewering of all things suburban are lost on them then there's no point in trying to explain. It's like D&D kids and their addiction to Monty Python, especially when it comes to *Monty Python and the Holy Grail*. I don't like it, but those guys throw around that "'tis only a flesh wound" line like some sort of secret handshake that gets you into some superhero speakeasy in the back of a comic book shop. You're either in the club, or you're not, and the Cult of *FEM* is a small one indeed. Members are keenly aware that *FEM* was years ahead of its time.

I learned about *Flesh Eating Mothers* purely by accident one Friday late in 1988 when I stumbled across a review in *The Washington Post*. Like I said before, the title alone was intriguing. Enough so to keep reading. Up until that point the only reviewing I'd been exposed to were thumbs up or down, but here was something completely different—a reading of the film from a post-AIDS perspective that explored the film's themes of sexuality, fidelity, and familial taboos.

Think about it, here's a movie where the local stud is cheating on his doting wife with every middle-aged divorcee on the block. Somewhere along the line he picks up an STD that affects women only, turning them into disfigured cannibals with a taste for their own children. By the late 1980s AIDS had already gone from "that gay disease" to one spread predominately by promiscuous heterosexuals. Anything left swinging after the free-loving disco era was tamed, wrapped in rubber, and brought out only on special occasions as the safe sex era began to blossom. After seeing how AIDS and HIV were eating away at their victims, here was a movie that dared to ask "what if the disease didn't eat away at you, but made the host eat away on their children instead." This parallel, when spelled out so clearly, blew my teenage mind. *FEM* was officially a movie I had to see. It was something I knew I could learn from.

I wasn't prepared for what finally hit video. I didn't know movies could look so cheaply made. Or that they could rely so heavily on bad puns, non-actors, and animated cartoon effects. And I certainly didn't know that horror films could be so cheerfully giddy despite presenting a worldview that's bleak, bitter, and cynical. That's really what got under my skin—the irony of it all. It broke every Hollywood rule I'd accepted as the norm and left me seeking more.

It wasn't until years later that I saw the similarities between *Mothers* and Lansdale's *The Drive-In*. Both use horror conventions and an absurdist eye to skewer accepted societal customs. No cow is too sacred; both are equal opportunity offenders where everything from religion to law enforcement are seen as self-serving corrupt institutions that prey on the weak with a pack-like ferocity. And they're both riotously hysterical while spilling doom, gloom, and gore. Silly, but still riotously hysterical.

If it weren't for either one I'd never have learned to love trash cinema and certainly never would have spent hours scouring video stores for previously viewed sleaze no one else would be caught dead renting, much less buying. They were gateway drugs that lead to a downward spiral of toxic avengers, dismembered mamas, and Andy Milligan, and there weren't enough fixes come Friday night to satisfy the cravings. They were my game changers.

For Y'ur Height Only (1981)
by Brad Paulson

Love James Bond? Ever want to see a James Bond style movie with a dwarf? How about a Filipino dwarf? Aren't you tired of all those damn tallie Fabios playing Bond? Fabios like Brosnan, Craig, Connery, Moore, and that drunk guy George Lazenby? Sure, they all hold their own as far as the franchise is concerned. But for my money, they can't touch the super-suave, ass-whipping lady-killer with pepperoni-sized nipples that is Weng Weng.

My favorite part of a Bond movie is and always has been when he's inside the circle, walks slowly and confidently, then turns and shoots at the camera and the screen fills up with blood. As kids, my brother and I were glued to these intros. Right before the shot was fired, we'd quickly jump out of the way, pretending we were avoiding it in real life.

For Y'ur Height Only starts the same way as the Bond movies do, except Weng is standing still instead of walking. Right away, you know the movie is great because it treats us to a dwarf staring directly into the camera. I can think of no better way to open a movie. Even though it bears many similarities, *For Y'ur Height Only* is not an official Bond film. It is a straight up rip-off from the Philippines. The technical flaws and stilted dialogue are hard to overlook (for me, they add to the enjoyment of the movie), but it gives us everything it advertises itself to be and has a charming sense of humor to boot.

The plot involves a dwarf villain by the name of Mr. Giant who kidnaps a doctor. The great Weng Weng is sent to his rescue. Giant is an elusive dwarf who talks to people through a mirror so they can't see his face. Most of the thugs that work for him are puzzled by his Wizard of Oz-style presence (or lack of presence, I should say). Only one toady of Mr. Giant seems to actually be able to see him.

Dwarf lovers or even merely mild appreciators will be in awe of this movie as Weng demonstrates incredible athletic ability in the fight scenes, falls from heights that would kill tallies, uses an umbrella as a makeshift parachute, flies with a jetpack, disco dances, fires guns nearly as big as he is, etc. This is one secret agent dwarf that knows how to live life to its fullest. The filmmakers might not know how to turn in a seamlessly edited film but they sure as hell know how to maximize their dwarf production value. Weng is perfect for this franchise as he radiates likeability and a larger-than-life screen presence.

With his bowl/mullet cut and plethora of puppety expressions, Weng's more adorable than anything else. I stopped counting the amount of times he looked at the camera, so he may not have been the best listener but regardless, he more than earns his keep. He also proves to be a skilled martial artist.

Due to his size, he's able to utilize stealth to crawl under his enemies' legs, execute crotch attacks from below, apply precision kneecap strikes and flip over the backs of tallies. He's an incredibly acrobatic stunt dwarf. He's also able to hide in bushes with ease.

Aside from his physicality (every time he opens a door, he's never taller than the handle), the dubbing of his voice also cracks me up. It's Americanized and sounds a little nasally. It reminds me of the cartoon character Snagglepuss.

Weng also sports some pretty impressive gadgets supplied by his boss: a radio necklace, a ring that detects all poisons, a special made dwarf gun with a silencer, a dwarf hipster hat with a blade on it (à la Oddjob in *Goldfinger*), a blowgun pen, a belt buckle that cuts through steel bars and shades that aren't just for style. They function like X-ray vision does for Superman except Weng uses them to watch the office girls type in the nude. He covers his mouth after he looks, reacting to seeing something naughty (even though it was only their shoulders that were visible). Weng with his white suit and hipster hat is a pretty amusing sight to behold.

Sadly, these gadgets are in more abundance than the real James Bond gets. Especially in the newer films, since nowadays they seem to strip his character down to a Jason Bourne clone. *Skyfall* comes to mind when tallie Bond (Daniel Craig) is given a gun and a radio and told that's all he's going to have. I can't say I was very impressed with that decision.

It's also funny that one of the main thugs seems to have the voice of Lawrence Bender in *Reservoir Dogs* and the dubbing for most of the rest of the male leads sounds like they're trying to impersonate John Wayne. The filmmakers also must've thought that all thugs speak like 1930s gangsters because they use the era's terminology throughout the film, with laugh-out-loud results.

The filmmakers also didn't leave out the seductive power Bond has with women as every female who comes into contact with Weng seems absolutely taken with him. This is refreshing to see since it challenges the stereotype of women falling for tallies.

Combine all these elements together (along with a dwarf-on-dwarf showdown at the end) and everything adds up to perfect fodder for a midnight movie. This is a great flick to watch with a crowd and maybe if you're a guy and you're shorter than your date she'll challenge the stereotype as well. If Weng Weng can't work the magic for you, no one can.

Frankenhooker (1990)
by Brad Paulson

I bet the last thing Mary Shelly imagined when she was writing the classic *Frankenstein* was that someone would do a take on her story that involved hookers. Or, who knows? Maybe she was much more open-minded than I give her credit for. After all, Frank Henenlotter isn't the only one who's gone crazy with her tale. He does give us one of the more entertaining and wilder versions I've seen though.

This may also be the only movie to date that includes exploding guinea pigs and call girls as the result of lethal exposure to super crack. It also features a severed flying hooker leg (think of the eyeball in *Evil Dead 2* for an easy frame of reference) and female body part puppets. This distinct kind of craziness can only be seen in a Frank Henenlotter film. The man has a wonderfully twisted mind.

Frankenhooker starts out with a deranged youngster, Jeffrey Franken (in what looks like an auto mechanic's outfit) talking to a brain in a jar. The brain has a large eyeball smack dab in its center. For all you old school horror movie fans out there, this was based off the advertisements for *The Brain That Wouldn't Die*. Right off the bat, this movie is bizarre. Especially when Franken gives the brain a lobotomy after it doesn't move its eyeball on command. This does the job and the eye responds to the motions of Jeffrey's hand. Just when things are getting interesting, his fiancé's mother walks in and asks him if he wouldn't mind passing the ketchup.

For those of you who haven't seen this film, if you're wondering why this might sound a little strange, it's because the large eyeballed brain in the jar of gel that he's playing with is in the kitchen of his fiancé's parents' home.

Franken looks downright deflated. Here he was, having his crazy and carefree mad scientist moment, and he's abruptly snapped back into the real world. I don't know about you, but if my fiancé's parents walked in the kitchen and saw me playing with a large eyeballed brain, they may just ask me some questions. Like, perhaps, "Why are you playing with a human brain, son?" Or, maybe, "Where did you get that human brain, son?"

And why would they let him use their kitchen to do aspiring mad scientist experiments on in the first place? Better yet, why would no one at the barbecue even notice? This is the beauty of many 1990s movies. Rarely did the characters even acknowledge situations like this. They were just presented.

Adding to the pile of strange things in this movie is the fact that Franken is not your average, run of the mill nerd by any stretch of the imagination. He's more of a hipster with semi-decent social skills. In other words, he's a 180 from the character I would assume him to be in real life.

Patty Mullen plays his girlfriend, Elizabeth Shelley (see an on the nose pattern in the names here?). Not only is she hot, but she complains about how she's fat which is bizarre because in 1987 she was named *Penthouse* Pet of the Year.

Liz is a sweetheart, but she's a bit of a dim bulb. She gets herself run over by standing like a dummy in front of the lawnmower Jeffrey created as a gift to her father. Instead of ignoring several warnings from her beau, she turns around, looks at the lawnmower as it's roaring full speed ahead at her, throws her hands up in the air and screams. She accepts her more than avoidable fate like the helpless lemming she is. Give that girl a Darwin award! This prompts Jeffrey to become hyper-focused.

With a dead girlfriend, a job at Jersey Electric immersed in biotech know-how, Jeffrey doesn't waste one precious moment shedding a tear for his ex-loved one. Instead, he buckles down and damn near reaches Herbert West status as he plans how to bring his fiancé back. He's got her body parts but they aren't in good enough condition for reassembly as we learn from the news report on Franken's TV:

"In a blaze of blood, bones, and body parts, the vivacious young girl was instantly reduced to a tossed, human salad. A salad that police are still sadly trying to gather up. A salad that was once named Elizabeth."

The only body part that's left intact is Liz's head. Franken takes it out to dinner at his parents' garage, which he's modified into his own low rent mad scientist lab. Like a good nerd, he's even all dressed up for the occasion, announcing that there's a storm coming in just two days and then it's reanimation time! He shows her several different options of what her new body can look like and talks to her as if she were still alive.

Now that Franken's wined and dined the severed head of his ex, he still has to figure out where to get the body parts to bring her back. There's not much time left, since the storm is coming soon. Franken has to think fast. He does what any aspiring mad scientist would do to come up with an answer: gives himself a lobotomy with a drill. This prompts him to come up with the brilliant idea that the best place to get body parts with no questions asked is downtown where the hookers troll! I don't know why he had to put a drill in his head to come up with this idea, but what do I know? I'm not a mad scientist.

It doesn't take long before Franken finds what he's looking for and negotiates with a pimp named Zorro (yeah, I know) to get a couple of hot hookers sent over to his place the following night. While he's there, he scores some crack.

Franken goes back to the lab and decides the best and most painless way to kill hookers is to make a lethal batch of super-crack. Another quick drill to the head gives him all the justification he needs for this diabolical act.

"I'm not shooting anyone. I'm not stabbing anyone. I'm merely gonna place a lethal form of crack in their presence. They don't have to take it. No one has a gun to their head. If they don't want to do it, they can just say no."

Needless to say, this is probably the most bizarre reasoning for a homicide I've ever seen in a movie.

Franken tests out his super crack on a guinea pig with disastrous, yet victorious results. When the hookers arrive, he gets cold feet but they find his crack and the decision is taken out of his hands.

Having everything he needs, Franken heads back to the lab and gets to work. His project is successful and Liz is brought back to life. Yet, she's not quite the same. Her head bobs like a pigeon and she pimp slaps Jeff when he refuses her invitation for a date. She's got the head of his ex but now she's basically an amalgamation of all the girls.

She wanders off and does what hookers do best: turns tricks. Unfortunately for the customers, the sex turns out to be too intense and she electrocutes them to death right before they explode. Much like in Mary Shelley's classic which this movie is inspired by, the monster goes on a rampage and leaves a trail of bodies in its wake. All sorts of crazy stuff follows including a brilliant moment in which the miscellaneous body parts of dead hookers form into grotesque, killer *Basket Case*-style puppets. *Frankenhooker* is a must watch for cult movie fans and Frankenstein completists alike. I also find it to be the most entertaining of Henenlotter's movies.

As a side note, with all the severed head scenes in this film, not to mention mad scientist themes, I feel this movie would make for a great double feature with *Re-Animator*.

Glen or Glenda? (1953)
by Greg Goodsell

December 10, 1978. Writer-director-transvestite Edward D. Wood, Jr., evicted from his skid row Hollywood apartment along with his wife Kathy and their five dogs, has sought refuge in the home of actor friend Peter Coe. That morning he was discovered on his hands and knees in front of Coe's refrigerator, limply trying to make highballs with orange juice and vodka. That afternoon Wood joined friends to watch a ballgame on television. Excusing himself to lie down on his bed for a while, Wood was later found dead—the result of a massive organ failure from chronic alcoholism—a horrified expression on his face.

Far, far away from this sordid scene in California, at New York's Thalia Theater, midnight audiences are delighted by a quirky and offbeat film that has some tangential themes with the cult hit *The Rocky Horror Picture Show.* The film, Wood's *Glen or Glenda?* is likewise about transvestism. And stock footage of buffalo stampedes. And dream sequences involving whipping and bondage. And Bela Lugosi...

Such was the fate of the "world's worst director," Edward D. Wood, Jr. Even a big-budget biopic starring Johnny Depp and directed by Tim Burton would fail to put money in anyone's pockets. What remains of the man's life is a fascinating heritage of a handful of films, countless pulp sex paperbacks, and produced soft-core porno films to bemuse the public in the decades following his death.

Anyone reading this is probably familiar with Wood's *Glen or Glenda?* It has no less than two narratives to explain everything to the befuddled audience. There's Timothy Farrell as Dr. Alton, the rational man of psychology who describes and eloquently defends the practice of transvestism, i.e. wearing the clothes of the opposite sex. There's also horror movie icon Bela Lugosi, who jumps into the action to mutter about "the secrets of the ages." One of his final roles, this has proved to be a bone of contention for Lugosi's son, Bela Lugosi, Jr. Refusing to have his father's likeness licensed to anything related to Wood, Junior has frequently described the poverty row producer as a "user and a loser" who exploited his dad in his sad final days. Especially irksome to the younger Lugosi is the fact that today's mimics are more likely to quote his father's lines in this film—"Pull de string! Pull de string!"—than from his signature role of *Dracula*. "I bid you...welcome."

Glen or Glenda? tells the story of Glen (played by Wood) and his fiancée Barbara (Wood's then-girlfriend Dolores Fuller). Glen is struggling with his transvestite urges and secretly covets the angora sweaters that Barbara wears. Against stark, minimalist sets using the most unattractive actors—the genetic women on display here could actually pass for men in drag!—Glen eventually comes clean to Barbara, who hands him her angora sweater as a totemic symbol of the effort she will put into their unconventional relationship.

Unconventional for 1953 and still most unusual for the twenty-first century, as shown in the Burton biopic *Ed Wood, Glen or Glenda?* was originally commissioned by soft-core sex fetishist producer George Weiss, who had carved out a niche creating female wrasslin' pictures such as *Racket Girls* a.k.a. *Pin-Down Girls.* Intended to exploit the then-hot Christine Jorgensen sex change scandal, Wood would take Weiss's money and fashion a project much more in line with his personal interests. Horrified with the results, Weiss then dropped in some "square-up" footage by including unrelated footage of strippers, gropers, and exotic dancers into the already fractured narrative.

Like most sexploitation of yesteryear which had fallen out of favor with increasingly explicit features, *Glen or Glenda?* would become a forgotten film. In the numerous articles *Famous Monsters* would run on Lugosi, editor Forrest J. Ackerman would run the shot of Lugosi giving benediction to a befuddled Wood in the occult study as seen in the film. Even here, Wood couldn't catch a break. Ackerman would later take credit for being one of Wood's "illiterary" agents, saying that Wood "would never spell any word the same way twice."

Winning the adulation of camp followers after Wood was given belated notoriety from the Medved Brothers' "Golden Turkey" books, Glen or Glenda? is now frequently screened and appreciated. Never boring—something Wood's *Plan 9 from Outer Space* and *Bride of the Monster* can't claim—*Glen or Glenda?* can be appreciated on an entirely different level.

Back before it became the name of a celebrated rock group, the "velvet underground" was alive and thriving in the Eisenhower era. Homosexuals, lesbians, sadomasochists, and transvestites were as active as ever, but were driven to more clandestine modes of expression. *Glen or Glenda?* drops the viewer into another world—and was indeed the product of another world—where dressing in the clothes of the opposite sex could land someone in jail and homosexuality was still illegal in all fifty states.

Edward D. Wood, Jr., a former Marine who took to the trenches wearing frilly underwear beneath his military uniform, was a part of this scene, but served as a quirky, positive role model. Wood enjoyed dressing in feminine attire, but took pains to live as conventional a life as possible. Aside from his secret wardrobe, Wood was a hard-working, masculine, stand-up sort of gentleman. He took pains to show this in *Glen or Glenda?* Transvestites—and by extension those who pursue an alternate lifestyle of any creed or color—are not the shadowy perverts who threaten the status quo but are tax-paying, upright American citizens who live next door to you, pursuing what they consider happiness. A radical thought for the 1950s, the message is even more important in an era that is now struggling to recognize same-sex marriages.

In this fashion, there is still some value to be gleaned by this woebegone "Z" picture long after Wood would slip out of his nylon stockings and pumps.

Gore Whore (1994)
by Allen Richards

I wish Hugh Gallagher didn't give up moviemaking; he was the VHS era's answer to no-budget grindhouse auteur Andy Milligan. Their films might have been small, rudimentary, and exploitative, but they weren't so much a simple product of what came before as a reaction to it. In the same way that the Sex Pistols were a reaction to the sorry state of rock-and-roll in the glam years, Gallagher's films grew out of the watered down limpness of horror in the late 1980s and early 1990s that saw the beloved genre cranking out live-action cartoons rather than dangerous, deadly cinema.

Gallagher, the publisher of *Draculina* magazine, was onto something with his "Gore Trilogy." Those films pushed the boundaries of acceptable sex and violence by framing their transgressive nature as dark comedies, even when the plots revolved around corpse fucking. The most easily accessible of the series is *Gore Whore*, with its conventional *noir*-like plot revolving around science gone amok. But fear not, despite a straightforward, mainstream plot, this High-8 lensed production still features all the extreme gore and explicit nudity one expects from micro-budget horror.

Gore Whore seems to draw most of its inspiration from *Re-Animator*, the last great horror film of the 1980s. The two films feature a similar sense of morbid humor, and Gallagher even pays direct homage a time or two, the best of which I'll get to in a minute.

As I mentioned before, the plot is rudimentary at best. Checking in at just over an hour, Gallagher wastes little time getting down to business. Our protagonist, Dawn, brings a john home to shag a few dollars out of, but first she gives the audience a quick striptease that goes from zero to full-frontal in well under thirty seconds. She quickly gives the john an oral castration followed by the one-two punch of an oral decapitation. This opening sequence works on a number of levels. Rather than a tease of things to come, it's a double promise to the two types of intended audience members. First, to all the perverts who bought the movie hoping for some B-girl skin. Second, it's one to the gorehounds hoping for some extreme bloodshed. Despite delivering goods right up front, neither group has seen anything yet. Another way to interpret the scene is to view it as a visual pun that plays up the title.

We quickly learn the girl's name is Dawn, and that she's a dead streetwalker brought back to life via a glowing, green re-animating agent. After escaping from the lab with a supply of green goo, the mad scientists out to find her hire a low-rent private investigator, Chase, who is dealing with the death of his wife. It's pretty easy to track down the trail of bodies Dawn is leaving behind, but Chase is in for a surprise when he finds out how the goo is administered. In Dawn's case, as she needs regular doses to keep going, it's vaginally. She sports a big old hypodermic needle with an even bigger cock attachment for insertion. In case you're wondering, yes, guys get it in the ass. It's a novel commentary on the idea in feminist film theory regarding the phallic nature of the weapons used in slasher films and of the metaphoric rape of the victims, and another great visual pun slamming the idea.

From this point, the film races to a conventional climax that ends all too abruptly, but not before delivering a few more great visual puns, my favorite being the "jerk off" in a Volkswagen bug. The journey isn't as important as the fun getting there and Gallagher does his best to ensure that viewers have a good time. There are plenty of decapitated talking heads, dismembered body parts, flowing blood, and a wealth of skin, some of which is shot with a gynecological point of view. This is fun for the whole family.

That's not to say *Gore Whore* is lightweight; Gallagher has a point of view worth mentioning. As I stated above, the film is shot in a rudimentary style. To be more accurate, like a porno. Even the scenes are constructed as such. They play out in the simplest of fashions, be they gore or sex. First the obligatory introductions are made, then the clothes come off, and eventually things play out that lead to bodily fluids spurting, squirting, or both. It's as if Gallagher is deliberately blurring the lines between sex and violence. He treats them as one in the same—to spin an old phrase, one man's pain is another man's pleasure. Or, less tritely, the beauty of sexual congress is as dangerous as grievous bodily harm, and the destruction of another's life is as euphoric as sexual bliss.

At the same time, *Gore Whore* is a celebration of B-movie conventions and archetypes. We have a femme fatale who is as much in the mold of classic *noir* vixens as she is in the deadly dames of those low-rent DTV Andrew Stevens erotic thrillers. A hero that's as pulpy as Sam Spade, but with a backstory that's pure *Lethal Weapon*. The plot is all zombies and mad scientists, and only about two steps removed from the Nazi variety. Gallagher wears his inspirations on his sleeve, just like Milligan.

Unfortunately, also like Milligan, Gallagher's films are pretty hard to come by. Milligan had the unfortunate luck to fall victim to careless distributors who often melted the film prints down for their silver when a title was pulled from distribution. Gallagher seems to have kept his films out of circulation by choice. If you're reading this book and this essay in particular, I'm guessing you're a horror fan, and you know how fans love to rock the rumor mill. When *Gore Whore* was released in 1994, it was produced on consumer grade video, the highest quality of which was Hi-8 (S-VHS was harder to come by, and was considered "pro-sumer"). This analog format wasn't very forgiving in low lighting, and even less so in the deck-to-deck nature of editing. The final product was often rough, to say the least. Twenty years on, and the rumor mill spins a tale of Gallagher not believing the series had enough life in it, especially in its primitive format, to justify any sort of remastering. With the slow death of the DVD niche markets, he might be right, but the preservation of his work to a digital format is justifiable in a historical context when examining the worlds of DIY, SOV, and underground cinemas. Even a simple conversion of the duplication masters to digital would be a step in the right direction. Between his films and his mini-publishing empire showcasing micro-budget cinema, it's hard to picture the current state of video cinema without the assistance of Hugh Gallagher. It's like trying to tell the history of 42nd Street without mentioning Andy Milligan.

I Spit on Your Corpse, I Piss on Your Grave (2001)
by Allen Richards

The following is a quotation from Nick Zedd's *The Cinema of Transgression Manifesto:* "Intellectual growth demands that risks be taken and changes occur in political, sexual, and aesthetic alignments no matter who disapproves. We propose to go beyond all limits set or prescribed by taste, morality, or any other traditional value system shackling the minds of men… The will be blood, shame, pain, and ecstasy the likes of which no one has yet imagined… This act of courage is known as transgression."

Translation: every transgressive element put to film is an overt political act of rebellion against classical cinematic structure and technique.

This begs the question: can a film be transgressive if it's corporatist in nature? Can a film that's designed solely as a for-profit endeavor be rightly regarded as transgressive art rather than simple soulless, trashy exploitation? Just because one shocks an audience by violating good taste and social taboos doesn't mean there's any intellectual depth to the work on display.

That idea is why I find Eric Stanze's *I Spit on Your Corpse, I Piss on Your Grave* his most fascinating film. Conceived as the debut release for the Sub Rosa Extreme DVD line of explicit titles geared towards giving exploitation fans exactly what they crave and profiting directly from the exchange. Even Stanze describes it as his least impassioned work, essentially a work-for-hire gig, and seriously considered releasing it under a pseudonym. While the film might not be up to the standards Stanze holds himself to, it shouldn't be so easily dismissed by anyone.

Allow me to back up a minute and provide a little historical context. Former owner of Sub Rosa Studio, Ron Bonk, once told me that all one needed to get sales going for a title was to have "that one scene that gets people talking." Something so out there that the film had generated some sort of word of mouth. Even if the movie was terrible, people would be talking about "that one scene," and potential consumers are more likely to take a chance on a movie they haven't seen if they are at least familiar with the title. From that idea, the Sub Rosa Extreme label was born, and Stanze, known for his transgressive masterpieces *Ice for the Sun* and *Scrapebook*, was asked to oversee production of the titles, essentially creating a mini-studio system in the St. Louis region designed to mass-produce seedy no-budget releases—think Full Moon, only smaller.

Stanze didn't just give Bonk a single worthy scene, he packed *I Spit* with wall-to-wall vulgarity. To bring all this about, he enlisted Emily Haack, a fearless actress without an ounce of vanity whom he worked with on *Scrapebook*. Emily, always the best thing in every movie in which she appears, certainly isn't "stripper hot" like so many other "actresses" in the DIY scene, and by that I mean all silicon, plastic, and fake, but she's definitely a pretty girl whose security in her own natural beauty and sexuality make her all the more attractive. As an artist, Emily isn't afraid to use her body, or her acting partner's body, even in a sexual way, as a tool to craft a compelling performance. And, yes, this means acting in scenes that could be considered hard core but non-pornographic due to the context. To the best of my knowledge, she's only gone to these extremes in *Scrapebook* and *I Spit*. If you're familiar with *Scrapebook*, Stanze's best known release, then you undoubtedly remember the fellatio scene. While little more than a dick-lick, it was enough to stir discussion about that bleakest of films, cementing Bonk's belief in "that one scene."

I don't think even Bonk was prepared for the extremes Stanze and Haack were about to embark with *I Spit*, and especially not the sheer volume of them. There's a wealth of full-frontal nudity, both male and female, and with that comes explicit penetration, genital mutilation, sexual humiliation, urination, defecation, and oral regurgitation. I'm sure I'm forgetting a good number of other "-tions" that go hand-in-hand with this movie about rape, murder, captivity, and torture. In true Zedd style, *I Spit* certainly goes "beyond all limits set or prescribed by taste, morality, or any other traditional value system."

If *I Spit* simply presented its checklist of tastelessness, I'd be more apt to dismiss it as simple assembly line exploitation, but this exploration of rape-revenge conventions embraces another of Zedd's Manifesto credos—"a sense of humor is an essential element"—that take the work in a subversive direction. *I Spit* satirizes rape-revenge conventions by often presenting the revenge being the rape, but only when gender roles are reversed (I'd suggest this plays into certain feminist film theories, but that would run contrary to Zedd's Cinema of Transgression ideal of "openly renounc(ing) and reject(ing) the entrenched academic snobbery" supporting such insights). By exploring the genre's conventions in such a way, it could also be argued that Stanze is satirizing audience expectations as well. In this regard, it's not all that different from John Water's transgressive milestone, *Pink Flamingos*. Both films not only indict the audience for their voyeuristic intentions, but when catering to that audience, spin the delivery into something exceeding their expectations.

In what is arguably the film's most transgressive act, at least in regards to genre expectations, Stanze denies the audience the actual rape, and thus the cause-effect nature of the revenge. The initial sex scene, between Haack and Stanze himself, is a surprisingly tender moment—a reunion of old lovers enjoying each other's touch. Granted, the scene starts at knifepoint and ends in betrayal, but by removing the aggression from the congress, Stanze is effectively giving the finger to both the audience members and their carnal expectations. Even when crafting a film so simplistic in its glory and execution, Stanze refuses to curb his artistic rage. The actual rape of Haack's character, Sandy, sparking her revenge is something more metaphorical— a rape by all of male-kind as every man in her life sees her as nothing more than ample bosom, curvy ass, and easy virtue. Through a series of flashbacks, viewers see her debased by males in every social circle of her life, and the sequence even culminates in Sandy being date raped, but she's strong enough to transcend that act and becomes a survivor. It's more of a mental rape that pushes her into insanity, and then the taking of her revenge on her co-captives, who, coincidentally, are some of the men responsible for her anguish.

These are just some of the examples that could support this argument of the film's worth, and could be explored more in-depth through various avenues such as continuing to catalog every transgressive act in the film (of which there are many) to breaking down every one of Sandy's acts of revenge (perhaps cigarette burns to a phallus representing traditional vaginal tearing, or the bloody death by sodomy Sandy unleashes on one loathsome bastard) and relating them directly to Zedd's manifesto. At some point, I would love to see one of you readers disregard Zedd's *Cinema of Transgressive Manifesto* and explore the film through various feminist, sociological, or even historical film theories. My point in all this is that even when a film's director dismisses that film's value both artistically and economically, it doesn't mean it's any less viable and not worthy of study and discussion. *I Spit's* blatant commercialism isn't what weakens the film, but what makes it unique in Stanze's catalog. It's a clear case of a filmmaker personalizing an impersonal effort whether they're conscious of it or not. I, as a passionate viewer, just happen to see the film aligning politically with a specific cinematic movement, whether the filmmaker was conscious of it or not.

I Spit on Your Grave (1978)
by Allen Richards

Those gams. Boy, oh boy, those gams. That rump, too…

Summer 1985 and I'd just turned twelve but didn't own a VCR yet. That didn't stop me from swinging by the video store after my weekly excursion to the dollar movie at New Carrolton Mall—really a strip mall with one enclosed end that housed an AMC multiplex, Sears, a comic shop where I spent the rest of my allowance, and that video store. That video store was always the last stop before the two-mile walk back home. I can't remember the name, and the mall was razed years ago to make way for urban sprawl, but there was nowhere else where my prepubescent friends and I could get a look at some tit. Sure, the *Dawn of the Dead* box had some boobage, and the slack-ass working the register didn't seem to give two spits if we ducked into the Adult aisle for a minute or two, catching our first glimpses of Betamax beaver, but there was just something about that *I Spit on Your Grave* box art that I couldn't help but keep coming back to. Oh, yeah, it was those gams. That rump, too.

It would be years before I'd finally get around to watching the actual movie. Two-and-a-half years later my family finally got their first VCR, and sometime around then I'd gotten into reading *Fangoria* and *Gorezone*. While my horny little ass should have been all over that rental, I'd built it up to be some sort of exploitation holy grail that I'd have to work my way up to. There were a few movies like that, ones I was too afraid to rent after reading the hype in *Fango—The Evil Dead, Faces of Death, Make Them Die Slowly*, and *Burial Ground* come immediately to mind. By the time I was able to muster the sack to pluck down for *I Spit* in the spring of 1991, I'd been rendered catatonic by *Evil Dead* the year prior, and spent a night trying to keep down a wave of up-chuck after one of my sister's freshman, teenybopper gal-pals brought over *Burial Ground* (for the record, the gore effects didn't get to me, at least not that much, but that weird hausfrau chowing down with her mouth open still makes me want to wretch twenty years later).

In those days I rented some real garbage. "Safe" horror title— ones that didn't carry those "Banned In X Number of Countries" warnings. While I don't remember that exact warning on the *I Spit* box, I'd finally gotten to the point where everything outside of those gams wasn't lost on me. Words like "raped," "burned," and "mutilated" were my warnings. So was Roger Ebert's review in his 1990 *Movie Guide.* What he depicted was something so vile that I was assured to again be rendered a little screaming bitch, just like I was during *Evil Dead.* Simply put, I just never had the stones to pluck down.

The only reason *I Spit* even made it into my house at all was that school let out early one day. That close to graduation, half days were common, and I remember thinking that if I were ever going to watch this fucker, it had to be then. That day—"just do it and get it over with." While it was sunny out—to avoid another midnight *Evil Dead* meltdown. Before my mother came home from work— the promise of full 1970s bush was something you never wanted to let your mother catch you indulging.

Strangely, while I remember events leading up to the movie as if they happened yesterday, the movie itself is little more than a blur. Hell, I remember more of what I thought about the movie as it unfolded than I do the movie itself. Sure, images come to mind, but they're more like random flashes. Camille Keaton holding that ax above her head as that raging speedboat roared the ultimate "I am Woman" message with so much finality that Gloria Steinem could have given up her crusade and just plastered a frame grab on billboards across the country and men the world over would have been rendered instantly impotent.

The campout. God, that campout. Every bit as poorly written and embarrassing to watch as Ebert said. But, as fate would have it, that "do you think girls poo?" discussion echoed exactly what one of my redneck friends stated to me only weeks prior. Apparently, pretty girls dropping deuces is about as hard to fathom as, say, why anyone would stick their dick in a blender. Is there some sort of extra taboo associated with a dirty human function if the participant is lust worthy? Was it just some sophomoric idiot's attempt at lame potty humor? I still don't know, nor do I care, but just the same, I'll never forget that campfire discussion, or my redneck friend wondering the same thing in earnest, or thinking "Holy Jesus, Ebert was right!" While on the subject of potty humor, there's the film's sole bathroom scene and another disconnected image burned right into my brain where Camille emasculated one of her attackers (and every audience member harboring lascivious thoughts) while he took a bath. The punishment certainly fit the crime, but to a teenager who hadn't actually put his to proper use yet, this seemed by far the most heinous act of the entire film.

Then there's Camille Keaton herself. She did indeed look gorgeous, especially naked, and that's really all I remember about the thirty minutes of rape. Rape, as a concept and not just a cinematic convention, was completely alien to me then and I'm not sure exactly how that early exposure might have affected me over the years but somewhere along the way, either as it unfolded before me then or in the twenty years since, I've pretty much forgotten/repressed the bulk of the film's rape. Just a single image of Camille is all I can muster, but that might have more to do with that exact image being posted all over the fanboy driven Internet than it does my recall ability. Watching the *I Spit* remake recently, I was able to connect certain scenes to moments in the original, but drew a complete blank during the scenes of rape. Was it too traumatic for me then? Was the embarrassing possibility of being titillated during the exposure too humiliating to remember? I'm tempted to say "no" on both simply because of my reaction during the closing credits, when I thought, "Really? That was it? What was all the fuss about?" In hindsight, that might be my most disturbing memory of the film and the reason I've never been tempted to watch it since. Then again, just today I picked up the DVD case at Best Buy and gave the once over, once again, to those gams. That rump, too.

Ilsa: She Wolf of the SS (1978)
by Jess Hicks

I can sum up my love for horror and exploitation film in two stories. The first involves a very frightened 11-year-old watching *Nightmare on Elm Street*, and the second involves a very, we'll say…fascinated, 16-year-old watching *Ilsa: She Wolf of the SS*.

At sixteen, I really dove into the world of horror; I wanted to consume as much as humanly possible. I didn't drink, smoke, or do drugs…hell I didn't even drive! What I'm saying is I was the world's most boring teenager, so to fill that void where there should have been debauchery, I instead filled it with movies; movies filled with sex and violence and all the other good stuff any other self-respecting teen would seek out.

So I turned to the Internet and signed up for Netflix and my whole world opened up with a bang! One perk of being a teen in the 2000s was the limitless amount of technology at my fingertips. I could find any movie I wanted and even more that I didn't know existed. The unofficial Netflix forum was my main source of information and led me to the very movie I have chosen to speak about in this book. I met friends in the Exploitation group that I still talk to today. They introduced me to hundreds of movies I never even knew existed, in particular Nazisploitation. I couldn't believe there was a sub-genre dedicated to Nazis. After some digging I not only found out this sub-genre was wildly popular, but it also seemed to be a sort of rite of passage for any self-respecting fan of trash cinema. I had to see it!

Ilsa: She Wolf of the SS was the obvious choice for me because it seemed to have the biggest following and seemed the most perverse. If you're unfamiliar with *Ilsa*, all you need to know is she is portrayed by blonde bombshell Dyanne Thorne and is the most evil woman you could imagine. She uses women as test subjects for electric shock dildos and castrates any man who can't please her sexually (basically all of them). Perhaps at sixteen I shouldn't have been watching such diabolical trash, but what did I care? I had a cavalcade of filth to watch and I was determined to inhale all of it as quickly as I could.

On one fateful Saturday I invited two friends over for pizza and movies while my mom was out. A seemingly innocent night. So we hid away in the basement where I had an ancient couch and giant tube TV to watch whatever had arrived from Netflix that day. By a twisted turn of events, *Ilsa* had shown up on my doorstep in all her Nazi glory. I loaded the disc and sat back with my friends for what would be one of the most uncomfortable ninety minutes of my life. I sat with my friends as Ilsa performed vile experiments, forced men to fuck her and even pee on another Nazi officer. The movie ended, the credits rolled, and I was a different person. I wanted more of this disgusting, filthy trash!

I owe *Ilsa: She Wolf of the SS* a lot. It inspired me to seek out more like it and branch out in all directions of film. It made me the "movie" person of my group of friends. (I was the one people asked to show them weird shit.) It, ultimately, brought me here to write this essay along with many other writings. I still continue to seek out the strange trashy cinema in the darkest corners of the world, and I will do so until I die. But Dyanne Thorne will always stick with me as my first venture into this world and one day I will go to Vegas with my fiancé and we will get married by Dyanne Thorne.

Oh, and my friends who I watched *Ilsa: She Wolf of the SS* with? They were not bitten by the bug like I was, but deep down they wanted a little more. I still get texts every once in a while reminding me of that day.

Killer Klowns from Outer Space (1988)
by Christopher Morley

Step into the big top and prepare to be dazzled by circus life imitating art—or is it art imitating life? Ever since my first exposure to *Killer Klowns from Outer Space* as a naïve student, I could not help but wonder, and now, as a naïve older writer, I'm still pondering. Consider its background—directed by special effects wizards the Chiodo Brothers, it could be as much a love letter to the circus arts as an all-too visceral reminder of their dark side.

Rather wonderfully, the circus enters town as a neat spin on the classic "crashed spacecraft" trope, curiosity getting the better of farmer Gene Green (an easy day's work for the magnificently named Royal Dano). He and his dog meet a nasty end at the hands of the titular Killer Klowns, red-nosed harbingers of doom who make it their self-appointed mission to find ever more ridiculous ways to dispatch victims; the popcorn gun and candy cocoons are among some of the macabre delights peddled by these slapstick sadists.

If that weren't enough to put you off a trip for life, that most basic of clownish tricks, the balloon animal, is also put to frighteningly clever use as a sort of hunting dog—and all of this inside the first few minutes!

The strange mix of fear and enjoyment, which can interchange throughout a viewing experience such as this, reaches fever pitch once the line between comedy and horror has been somewhat blurred. It reaches a crescendo as the Klowns spread their net wider, putting shadow puppetry, rubber mallets, pies to the face, and overlong boxing gloves to over-the-top use.

Are we to laugh or recoil in terror? Or both? You'd be forgiven for throwing your popcorn to the floor (if it's survived past the showmanlike reveal of some similar-looking baby Klowns whose diet appears to consist solely of shrunken people) and cursing the name of Philip Astley forthwith (the man widely credited with the introduction of what we would nowadays recognize as the circus into popular culture).

But a glance even further back reveals that the Ancient Rome origins of the spectacle could be every bit as horrifying as what you're being shown on screen, and equally as alien, so think before you spit out your drink, even if you may want to following the revelation of just how the Klowns drain their victims—it involves a straw...

If you're reading on, still humming Julius Fucik's "Entrance of the Gladiators" to yourself (arguably the definitive entry in anyone's list of circus music), you'll be pleased to know that the sound-world is every bit as important as its cinematic cousin.

Composer John Massari excels in creating a score that is equal parts daft and diabolical, the contrast between sound and vision at key points in the narrative undeniably more shocking than the acting and dialogue, the real clue as to the more practical origins of its directors.

And if you yourself or anyone you know suffers from a fear of circuses, exposure to this film will either cure or increase it, laughter at the ridiculousness of it all or utter terror after stumbling across some unpleasant visual cue to bring back the repressed inherent darkness of your first visit to the big top being the two ends of the spectrum. Perhaps the best way to ease them, and yourself, into the experience is to treat it as exactly that which it seeks to turn on its head—a circus show.

After all, thrills, spills, popcorn, knowingly hammy acting, musical cues by turn terrifying and an open invitation to giggle—a definite common lineage bridges the gap between circus and cinema in this case, and it's not too hard to suspend your disbelief if you throw yourself into it either.

A rough "trick-reveal-death-trick-reveal-death" pattern quickly makes itself known, and coincidentally you can indeed mentally hum the structure to yourself to the rough tune of the aforementioned "Entrance of the Gladiators," as well as adding tuneful admonishments to the characters on screen not to investigate what's going on at the none-too-subtly named "Top of the Hill" make-out point, or the

"Klown Kathedral." Quite why our genocidal jape-merchants require one is never really explained until we meet Jojo the Klownzilla, a giant Klown who clearly fulfills the role of Pope to the Kathedral's kongregation.

Anyone expecting a sermon on faith, hope, or charity and a few hymns will be wishing they'd stayed tuned to Songs of Praise once they realize his intentions—following the rescue of Debbie (a superbly screamy Suzanne Snyder) by the Terenzi brothers (Michael Siegel as Rich, alongside Peter Licassi's Paul) by a well-aimed ice cream van, he manifests as a giant puppet and quickly breaks free of his strings, intending to gobble anyone vaguely human for himself.

Luckily for most of the gang of teenage stereotypes, he gets a mere snack instead of his intended full-blown supper, the Terenzis managing at least to appear to die with some measure of honor without having to leave their van.

As ever with the performing arts, though, nothing is quite what it seems, a twist of fate and a good place to hide sparing them the ignominy of a "death by Klown" entry in the obituaries section of the local paper. It can't happen twice, though, can it? Sheriff Dave Hanson (John Allen Nelson), having overcome initial skepticism to come to the hilariously-monikered Mike Tobacco (Grant Cramer)'s aid when the circus literally came to town, also appears to bite the big one in this dogfight which returns their small town to its normal Klownless self, but somehow survives—a piece of trickery equally as confounding as any equivalent an experienced clown could pull from his inevitably very small bag.

Just to seal the deal, the convoluted ending is a masterful nod to the very basic DNA of clowning—"is it over?" quickly followed by a shower of pies and an evil laugh. Over to you, *Cirque Du Soleil*...

Lady Terminator (1989)
by Chris Watson

Seldom can one role define someone's career, but that's the case with Barbara Anne Constable. Barbara played the lead in *Lady Terminator*, blowing away male genitalia with a vengeance. The Indonesian film was a box office smash before being banned. The film garnered word of mouth from websites and magazines, building the movie's popularity. For instance, Jose Prendes of StrictlySplatter.com wrote, "There will never (ever, ever) be another movie on StrictlySplatter.com that tops the insanity from start to finish that this amazing movie manages to pull off with flying colors. Constantly hilarious and entertaining, this is a shining example of bad movies (which works in its favor) making it a pure and undeniable work of art." *Lady Terminator* amassed such a following that the movie continues to screen in an abundance of packed theaters worldwide.

Barbara was born in London, England, but grew up in Brisbane, Australia, where she experienced "a lot of domestic violence and alcohol issues" over the course of her childhood. At fifteen, Barbara began modeling, getting her start in bridal magazines. Eventually modeling led to acting. Before landing her most famous role, the modeling led to a bit part in a Hong Kong movie. Barbara visited modeling agencies in Hong Kong. One agent submitted her for a film that would become *Lady Terminator*.

Barbara auditioned and received the role. Barbara said, "I was just modeling. I had some acting experience, but could never afford to be an actor. The role didn't require a lot of speaking, but did require a lot of physical endurance. I had to look a certain way and was very fit." Perhaps the biggest hurdle for any actress interested in the role is the nudity and violence. In terms of the nudity involved with *Lady Terminator*, however, Barbara was more than comfortable. As a model, she appeared in an overseas version of *Penthouse*. On nudity, Barbara stated, "I always had a freedom with my body. I never had an issue with being in the nude. We're born in the nude. When you're dancing, you're in leotards and short-shorts and little tops. You're constantly rehearsing with next to nothing on anyway. Everybody around you is the same. When you're doing shows, you have so many costume changes within a two hour show that you're ripping your clothes off and running around with no clothes on, so is everybody else. You become accustomed to it. That's part of it. Also, I think it's because athletes have incredible bodies. They know they look good and don't feel self-conscious about their body."

The flawless nudity would make the movie all the more memorable, but she was also required to carry around giant weaponry and blow away crotches. With the high level of violence comes the need to use weapons, but the star of the film had never fired a gun before. Barbara says, "When I first arrived, they gave me a workshop. It was an Army guy that showed me how to load, reload, shoot, target, aim, and fire. When you fired, you really had to have a good hold of it. Otherwise, it knocked you around. That's the only time I ever shot guns before or since." After training, the star of the film began blowing away men. The majority of the kills involve crotch violence.

The film, especially the first half, is littered with phallic symbols. When asked about all these symbols, Barbara recognized their significance, stating, "The big erect cock is the symbol of manhood. I suppose in the film, it was masculinizing me. The power of the cock was transferred to me. I was having their cocks ripped off, shooting them off. The symbolism is wrapped up in that." However, the symbolism and creative deaths were not all in the script. Instead, they came from the mind of director H. Tjut Djalil. The film became about obliterating the men. Barbara says the male-directed violence "wasn't so much in the script as in the direction. He wanted those deaths to be brutal." Djalil uses a similar style in his other films.

The violence played a strange role in not only the movie but also Barbara's personal life. In response to the violence in the film, Barbara stated, "I've had a lot of anger toward men. I still do have the anger. I wrote a book on domestic violence when I came back from Hong

Kong in my twenties. My first serious relationship from about age nineteen to twenty-five was with a guy who started beating me up. When I did *Lady Terminator*, it was easy for me to do because it was a cathartic experience. It helped me to kill all these men. I was able to get rid of all that rage, and do it in a safe way. There's definitely a lot of anger and rage that I directed in that character. That's why it was so easy for me to play that character." Although the movie was a "joke" to the lead actress, she was able to wrestle with her demons and gladly take her $30,000 paycheck.

Many film fans will mention *Lady Terminator* as a female-starrer that borrows heavily from *The Terminator*. While enough is changed in the stories, to name a few notable similarities is not difficult. For instance, both films include the quiet killer at the helm, the mass killing scene, and the infamous eyeball scene. At the time, the knock off concept was not unusual. 1983's *Hundra* featured Laurene Landon as a female Conan character. Both *Hundra* and *Lady Terminator* had a Roger Corman and, later, Asylum Entertainment knock-off schlockiness to them, but they become something special by switching the lead to a female. With any female action hero comes the discussion of feminism. These two films are prime examples of how Hollywood saw female action heroes. The Hollywood studio versions each feature a masculine male. The independent films feature women.

Lady Terminator, in particular, seems filled with attempts at feminism. For instance, the previously mentioned phallic symbols surrounding her before she becomes a masculine murderer. Also, there's even the classic line, "I'm not a lady. I'm an anthropologist." While the line gets laughs in theaters for its over-the-top nature, it has a lot more to say than what's on the surface. When asked about the line, Barbara replied, "I think what she was trying to say was, 'Don't call me lady because I'm not. I'm not a vagina. I'm a true professional. Just because I'm female, you keep calling me lady. I'm actually an educated woman.' It's again about a woman standing up for her rights and equality."

In the film, the well-educated woman would eventually become possessed and raging crotch violence would begin. Barbara "relate(d) to her shooting the cocks off. The correlation for me is that a strong woman killing men, shooting their cocks off, is what a lot of women really wish they could do to certain men." Whether you're looking at feminism as equality for all or women conquering all, this film has it.

The star of *Lady Terminator* would do her best to forget the film that personally "empowered" her. Like many actors from cult films, the movies get hidden away and, often, forgotten. A good example can be seen in a story filmmaker Jack Hill told during an interview. He ran into an actor a few years after they worked together. The actor was very embarrassed by the movie they made together. Twenty years later, the movie is a cult hit. Jack goes to a convention and sees the actor selling photos from the movie. Likewise, Barbara thought *Lady Terminator* was "fucking crap" and looked "amateur" when she first saw it. Despite the box office success, even the star's copy of the film was stored away and forgotten.

Unfortunately, the film was banned in Indonesia and seemed lost. Barbara never thought the movie would be seen again, let alone become a cult classic. Luckily, the movie continues to be seen at midnight showings and revived releases. With its success has come its acceptance from the star. She has shown the film to her family and friends, has accepted numerous interviews, and has appeared at *Lady Terminator* events. The over-the top-violence, bad acting and dialogue is comical in its absurdity. When a viewer is able to accept that, you get an addictive, trashy treat.

The Last House on the Left
(1972)
by Tim Ritter

*Keep repeating…it's only a movie, only a movie, only a movie… Can a movie go too far? Mari, seventeen, is dying. Even for her, the worst is yet to come…*There we have it, just a small sampling of some of the lurid taglines used in prints and advertising to entice the movie-going public into seeing Wes Craven's now classic first feature film, *The Last House on the Left.* What is it about this movie that made it a cult classic? Why do some fans hate it so much while others embrace it so readily? What is it about *The Last House on the Left* that has made it endure so long…going into five decades now? Who knows for sure? I can only give my perspective on things and why it caught my fancy as a young teen horror fan and burgeoning moviemaker. Amazingly, the movie has stuck with me decades later, and I continue to study it and homage it in almost every movie I make, in one form or another. I also watch it religiously at least a few times each and every year.

When *Last House* was in its original run, mainly at drive-ins and grindhouse theaters across the U.S. in the early and mid-1970s, I was just five or six years old, so, of course, I missed all that firsthand action. There was outrage and controversy; theater owners and projectionists snipping scenes out of the movie that they deemed offensive…sex and violence sequences that had gone *way too far…* all of which led to big box office returns (over time) and plenty of notoriety. There was also wild documentation of the reactions from the staggered public who had been lucky enough to see the movie when it played in theaters, with most of them allegedly ending up in a stunned shock, vomiting in their seats, or fleeing from the cinema in pure terror when things just got too intense. The people

I came across who had actually *seen* the film rarely wanted to talk about it, and when they did, it was *never* in a favorable light. They spoke of the experience almost as if they had accidentally attended a black mass, like the movie was heretical. One guy told me, "There ought to be laws against filming anything like that." It was nonstop tales like these that continued to fuel my imagination regarding all things *Last House on the Left* for at least five years or more. Endless questions bounced through my mind... *What could this movie possibly be? Was it snuff? Would I ever get to actually see it in any form?! How far could a movie legally go? And how about all those early titles that the movie wore—Krug and Company...Sex Crime of the Century...* What did they all mean? Why were there so many cuts of the movie? Everything about *Last House* was just an enticing obscurity, something that was constantly just out of my reach, and as a card-carrying horror fanatic, I needed to find out so much more about it...by experiencing it firsthand somehow.

The storyline for *Last House* is pretty simple: Mari (Sandra Peabody) and Phyllis (Lucy Grantham), two hip, free-spirited, 1970s gals just entering young womanhood, head to the big city for a night on the town. They are celebrating Mari's birthday. They see a hard rock group named *Bloodlust* (that seems inspired by Ozzy or Alice Cooper from that era) and after the concert, they try to score some pot in a seedy part of town. The guy selling the grass is affiliated with a group of criminals that just broke out of jail (for, among other things, killing nuns and priests as we hear in an early radio news blurb.). The group of thugs, which includes leader Krug (expertly played by David A. Hess), Weasel (F.J. Lincoln), Sadie (Jeramie Rain), and Krug's son Junior (Marc Sheffler), kidnap the girls, throw them in a car trunk, then take them out into the woods where they sexually assault and slowly murder them in cold blood. Making for a getaway, the criminal vermin discover their car has broken down out in the middle of nowhere and they head over to get assistance from a nearby house...which happens to be occupied by Mari's parents, Mr. and Mrs. Collingwood, who are anxiously awaiting her return from the extended birthday night out on the town. As a matter of fact, Mr. and Mrs. C. are more than a little upset about their daughter—they've contacted the police about her late return and are worried sick about her. When they ascertain that the rather peculiar characters staying in their house raped and murdered their daughter, they take the law into their own hands and kill off the group one by one, using chisel, chainsaw, electrocution, castration, and knives.

Growing up with *Fangoria* magazine, of course I knew who Wes Craven was, and by the time *A Nightmare on Elm Street* delivered the perfect theatrical boogeyman goods in 1984, I was a diehard fan of the man and his work, mainly from reading interviews and articles about his movies. I just couldn't get enough information about Craven and his work. As renting videotapes became mainstream and all the rage, I anxiously awaited for distributors to release some of the classic movies I had been reading and daydreaming about for so many years, including *The Hills Have Eyes* and *The Last House on the Left*. *Hills* came out first and did not disappoint. It was raw, intense, and spectacular! *Hills Have Eyes 2* hit the theaters as *Nightmare on Elm Street* made the regional theatrical rounds, and I enjoyed both of those flicks immensely. (I had just gotten my driver's license and guess where I'd make "practice runs" to every weekend? That's right, any theater showing *Nightmare* or *Hills 2*!) Craven was, no doubt, a master. But where was *The Last House on the Left*, this "Video Nasty" that had been banned in so many parts of the country and the world? This celluloid atrocity that angry and offended exhibitors had taken scissors to without the filmmakers' consent? The movie that Craven himself had intended to be XXX-rated in the beginning, and had written and shot much of it that way, but later had a change of heart (or felt immense guilt) and trimmed a lot of the material down himself before it was released. *What was left of this movie? Would it see the light of day again?*

Finally, in mid-1985, Vestron Video released *The Last House on the Left* on videotape, and I was there in my local mom-and-pop video store day and date to rent a copy of this bad boy of cinema. As a matter of fact, I had *reserved* a copy of it months in advance.

Finally sitting down and watching *The Last House on the Left* on video for the first time was an exhilarating experience! Near life-changing! The good girls going bad—and being punished! The sex! The violence! The revenge! The bizarre music, which included folksy ballads during moments of sadness (along with some of the first-ever synthesized electronic stingers), all performed by lead baddie Krug himself, David

A. Hess. Then there were the oppressive song lyrics that I couldn't get out of my mind, no matter how hard I tried: "And the road leads to nowhere." Haunting and perfect. And let's talk about Krug/Hess himself—he was *scary*. It was hard to decipher (at first) whether or not this individual was really an actor or perhaps a crazed psychopath that the filmmakers broke out of jail and followed around, filming his crimes as they went along. And wow, the iniquitous ending, where the parents extract their revenge upon the sex maniacs, was just as intense as I'd imagined it would be, including the notorious, much ballyhooed sequence where Mrs. C. fellatios Weasel and then chomps it off! *And justice was served…*in a way that was just so extreme it was hard to believe that, "yep, there it was, right on my television screen!" Can't forget the nice liberal use of a chainsaw by Mr. C., either, two years before Tobe Hooper released his massacre with the aforementioned tool. There was also Craven's early use of "booby traps in the house," which *The Hills Have Eyes* and *Nightmare on Elm Street* brilliantly expanded on, but there was something just *right* and *retro* about seeing the 1970s' humble beginnings of these "fighting back" concepts in *Last House*. It was also cathartic to see the "eye for an eye, tooth for a tooth" ending with the parents getting justice when the inept law could not.

There was the shaky, documentary-like style of the movie, which made it seem so real. The grainy look of the picture, which resembled something a VHS video camera might deliver at the time. And the sex and the violence, which I had read about for so many years by then, that my mind kind of filled in the blanks, probably supplying amply exaggerated substitutes for anything unseen. Somehow, I *was* seeing it all, and more! That's the thing about hype, suggestion, obsession, and nostalgia; I was so worked up to see this film that just enough was onscreen for it to deliver in a powerful and hypnotic way that I had yet to experience in a horror movie, at least not since seeing *Jaws* as a super young lad or *Halloween* a few years prior on NBC television.

Being an aspiring filmmaker myself, I absorbed the *Last House* ambiance and vibe like a sponge. Nothing went unnoticed—the microscopic budget, a "classic, well-known movie" filmed regionally, in the middle of Nowhere, Connecticut, as opposed to Hollywood, California. Special effects that weren't so special, but that were completely homemade and edited just fast enough to be impacting when needed. No need for the killer(s) to wear a rubber mask like in *Halloween*—it was quite the revelation to witness that the "bad guys and girls" looked just like you and me! (Saves on the budget, too—fewer props to buy.) Heavy use of outdoor sets like...*the woods*. Protracted, running chase scenes in those woods. Shaky camerawork and long, uninterrupted takes. The fact that there were no name stars or anyone I had ever heard of starring in the movie. The amateurish, murky photography, which made me feel like I had a chance to deliver something of similar, or maybe, if I was lucky, even *better* quality and get some sort of notice. The way the movie *did* go too far—I could tell there was a lot cut out (from both censors and auteur guilt), especially from the assault scenes—but the way Craven had reeled things in with choppy cutting and glaring continuity errors somehow transcended reality and took it to an audacious new level. Your mind filled in for missing reels. This was reality style in its rawest form and made you see and feel the evil actions even if they weren't exactly there on the screen 100%.

There was also the way the cast and crew had come together like a family to make the movie, using producer Sean Cunningham's family homes and backyards for many of the sets. The way talented musician and actor David A. Hess had played a lead role so menacingly in the movie and also delivered the soundtrack score—an invaluable practice, because being on the set every day and experiencing the making of the movie firsthand gave him such personal insight into everything that it led to an inconceivable creative energy for his scoring sessions, and he managed to find an incredible soul for the film with his contributions. His music is a timeless work of art in my book, and it shows—to date, it's been released three times as a standalone soundtrack score!

And I can't forget the iconic moments in the movie—the "in the truck" point-of-view shot looking up at the baddies when they pop the trunk of their car open to yank their victims out—how many filmmakers have borrowed this shot or technique since Craven trailblazed it with such great effect in *Last House*? Or the wickedly nasty introduction Krug has, walking past a child on the street and nonchalantly popping the kid's balloon with his trademark cigar. So disgusting and hilarious at the same time!

With regard to story and scripting, the importance of having interesting characters and great plot twists in your tale to keep the audience watching and, of course, the heavy use of near slapstick comic relief when dealing with such dark material and subject matter. I know some fans loathe the humorous moments of the cops making so many stupid mistakes and being about twelve steps below the intelligence level of Sheriff Rosco P. Coltrane from *The Dukes of Hazzard*, but their purpose is to give us a nice pressure release valve from the horrible proceedings we're being forced to witness as helpless voyeurs.

Finally, Wes Craven's *The Last House on the Left* showed me that the success of stylized no-budget exploitation *depends* on a small, dedicated cast, very little money, a tantalizing title, a balls-to-the-wall marketing campaign, and strong word-of-mouth. With those ingredients in place, not only can you make something impacting, you can make something that nearly transcends time and space and becomes legendary. That in itself is an inspiring cosmic revelation, and I'm still trying to come close in my own work to the zenith of perfection that Wes Craven's little grindhouse epic *The Last House on the Left* represents.

Manos, The Hands of Fate (1966)
by Rob Craig

Manos, The Hands of Fate is an excellent example of a throwaway cultural product which managed to outlive its original purpose to become a verifiable pop-culture icon. Shot at a remarkably low budget ($19,000) by an Texas entrepreneur who fancied himself a movie producer, *Manos* stands today as a premier example of a commercial film which, forgotten in its own time, gains stature exponentially as it ages, boasting an ever-increasing audience of (sometimes rabidly-devoted) fans, destined surely to become a timeless cultural artifact for the ages. After a disastrous "world premiere" in November 1966, and a limited regional release to theaters, *Manos* fell into obscurity until it was re-discovered in the early 1990s by Frank Coniff and showcased on a legendary episode of the cult television series *Mystery Science Theater 3000*. The astounding and utterly unique film then quickly joined the august pantheon of quirky, low-budget films derisively tagged as "the worst film ever made," and gained many devotees through this spurious but understandable classification.

Manos is, indeed, one of the cheapest films ever made. Shot silent on a 16mm newsreel camera with the voices rather crudely over-dubbed later, at times *Manos* looks like little more than an elaborate home movie from some enterprising film hobbyist. The acting, although adequate, tends towards the over-wrought and theatrical, understandable since the filmmaker recruited most of the main roles from the local community theater group. The grim real-life settings of *Manos*, including a creepy homestead and desolate expanses of desert, evoke a harsh, even hostile environment, which is entirely in keeping with the ultimately tragic scenario. *Manos* is amateur in the best, original sense of the word, a cultural product created by talented, enthusiastic non-professionals, made completely outside the established commercial film industry, and boasting none of that industry's slick look. So crude is *Manos*'s look, so primitive its singular verisimilitude, that in the *Mystery Science Theater* episode in which it is viewed, one character wonders if *Manos* is poised to turn at some point into a snuff film.

But as many (not all) of its fans have recognized, it is *Manos*'s very cheapness, its almost unbearably bleak minimalism, which makes the film so uncanny, so eerie, so memorable—and so unique. No other film ever made looks even remotely like *Manos*, an august achievement in an industry in which common production techniques and equipment impart a certain uniformity to even meager-budgeted film productions. Like other no-budget film geniuses of the time period, such as Ed Wood, Andy Milligan and Larry Buchanan, Harold Warren and company managed to fabricate a true nightmare fable out of the slimmest resources possible, creating a remarkable text that resonates more loudly with each succeeding generation of film lovers.

The synopsis for *Manos*, in a nutshell, sounds like any number of other films of the time period, and in fact is a standard horror trope: vacationing Suburbanites get lost in rural America and encounter scary backwoods predators. But here is where similarities end, because *Manos* takes this premise in a different direction than any other film. Warren and company's intention might have been merely to make a cheap horror film for fun and quick cash, but the resultant product reflects not only the peculiarities of the filmmakers but, most precipitously, profound socio-cultural forces abounding in the world at the time. 1966 marks the mid-point of a most astounding and tempestuous decade, with generational, political, social and aesthetic battles raging at all levels of society, and the incredible *Manos* manages to reflect many of these themes and conflicts, often in vivid relief.

Foremost of these is a brutal attack on the American family, drowning in the seductive vagaries of a decade of tumultuous upheaval. The impending collapse of morality which the "liberated" 1960s foreshadowed also invoked the ominous specter of political and societal anarchy, via the drug-and-sex revolution. Allied with these trends was the concurrent ascendancy of alternative religions, with Anton LaVey's "Church of Satan," founded in the very year of *Manos*'s birth, being the most ostentatious blueprint. Other topical themes addressed fleetingly, if vividly, in *Manos* are that of the relative merits of polygamy versus monogamy and the threat of staid suburban conformity being swallowed up by rural paganism. Indeed, *Manos* stands almost as a bizarre ritualistic destruction of the postwar American family, and its replacement by a bleak, amoral hippie commune, replete with torture, sexual perversion and hints of totalitarianism.

Although the nuclear family in *Manos* (father, mother, child, pet) is completely iconic and worthy of discussion in its own right, by far the most interesting character in *Manos* is Torgo, a bizarre flunky who "takes care of the place while the master is away." Looking equal parts hobo, drunkard, and mental patient, the shabby Torgo hilariously represents the service sector of Middle America, a most abstract sketch of the greeter or middle manager one might meet at a roadside Holiday Inn. Torgo is a hippie, a casualty of the free-love movement, drugged and full of abandon, but still a slave to his boss and his lower appetites. Torgo is bestial, half-civilized, half-savage, like one of Dr. Moreau's "manimals," deformed in body and deranged in mind, fit only for low, perpetually frustrated animal appetites, and/or dull servitude to stronger predators. In *Manos*, Torgo is an indelible symbol of libertinism, a sexual degenerate whose mental degradation and physical deformity are directly due to reckless, hedonistic living. (His mental and physical tics, in fact, suggest the ravages of an STD like gonorrhea). Torgo thus acts as cautionary tale for the inherent pitfalls of sex and drug abuse, two of the primary chimeras of the liberated 1960s. Torgo is, in essence, one of the earliest cinematic depictions of the hippie burnout, a cultural archetype which became ubiquitous in subsequent years. Torgo becomes even more iconic when one realizes that John Reynolds, the actor who portrayed the "hippie from another dimension," killed himself shortly after filming *Manos*; apparently Reynolds was a sensitive, creative soul who found modern life indeed unbearable.

Even today, *Manos*'s legacy grows exponentially. Several theatrical productions, including *Manos: The Rock Opera of Fate* and *Manos: The Hands of Felt*, pay dutiful homage to the film. Countless art projects—including drawings, paintings and sculptures—depict one or more *Manos* characters, with Torgo and The Master by far the most popular subjects. A recently-discovered 16mm work print unearthed by the film's original distributor and sold on online auction site eBay to film archivist Ben Solovey, has been painstakingly restored and the "new, improved" *Manos* boasts new 35mm theatrical prints, as well as a long-awaited Blu-Ray DVD release with commentary by several surviving participants. Indeed, as uncanny as *Manos* is, one is tempted to ponder the possibility that this utterly unique film, so unlike even its scruffy brethren in the trash cinema pantheon, exerts some sort of phantasmal influence on certain intelligent, creative souls, who seem drawn to the amazing film almost against their conscious will, to become willing disciples and devoted champions of one of the most extraordinary films ever made by a small group of dedicated non-professionals. In short, *Manos* is a prime example of a throwaway film that seems nonetheless destined to live eternally in popular culture.

Master of the Flying Guillotine (1976)
by Chris Watson

Jimmy Wang Yu is one of the most fascinating actors in Asian cinema. At times, one of the most popular actors, but his personal life is more interesting and made a life-changing impact on the path of his career. Wang Yu has been accused (and, in some cases, brags) of beating his wife, having affairs with directors' wives, bar brawls, and murder. On set, he was well known for making actual contact during fight scenes and stunts. Wang Yu may not have been the favorite of cast and crew members, but he built enough of a following that he was able to maintain a steady career. He launched to fame with *The One-Armed Swordsman*. The Shaw Brothers production would spawn sequels, including *The Return of the One-Armed Swordsman*, that also starred Jimmy Wang Yu. Unfortunately, Wang Yu broke his contract with the legendary Shaw Brothers, lost a lawsuit and was blacklisted. Wang Yu went to Taiwan to try and capitalize on his one-armed box office prowess.

Jimmy Wang Yu struck one-armed gold again when he teamed up with Golden Harvest for *One-Armed Boxer*. The story is about dueling martial arts schools. Everything changes when the villains hire a team of unique fighting professionals; they include Japanese karate experts, Thai kick-boxers, Tibetan Monks, and Indian Yoga experts. The team takes out all of Yu's school, but, unfortunately for them, they only karate chop off Yu's arm (you read that right and it happens not once but twice!). Obviously, the movie does get goofy at times. The team is purposely filled with distinct, oddball characters. Luckily, the movie makes up for the goofy moments with some pure badass moments. Yu's one-armed training sequence is the best. The determination Yu has to make his hand strong by consistent burning is cringe worthy, yet gives you an insane respect for his character. The dialogue doesn't disappoint either. Upon the first sighting of Yu, the villain says, "So, you're still alive." Yu answers stoically, "Hell sent me back." The version I saw topped it off by featuring a *Shaft*-like soundtrack.

Jimmy Wang Yu and David Chiang (Shaw Brothers's one-armed replacement star for Wang Yu) team up in 1976's *One Armed Swordsmen*. The two actors also team up to co-direct. Yu and Chiang know what their audience wants; the film features seven one-armed swordsmen. In the opening sequence alone, Yu slices off multiple men's arms. *One Armed Swordsmen* is filled with severed limbs, false arms, and one-armed fights—with and without weapons. The movie drags at times, but does feature a couple of large fight scenes. The difficulties of creating a flashy fight with one-armed characters are evident in this film. However, the film has a redeeming value that it probably didn't want. *One Armed Swordsmen* is simply absurd. The abundance of missing arms is one thing. The skill of all the one-armed characters is fine. What takes *One Armed Swordsmen* to a ridiculous level starts with absurd plot twists. Any viewer will be stunned by the plot revelations, but for the wrong reasons. The final fight scene tops it off—chickens are obviously thrown at the men as they duel. Imagine one of the many classic fight scenes with rain pouring, but replace the rain with chickens and you have the final fight scene of *One Armed Swordsmen*.

The year 1976 also brought *One-Armed Swordsman Vs 9 Killers*. Jimmy Wang Yu returns, but uses his fists against swords. The action is mindless in this one. The wonderful story of the Chang Cheh original is missing. Like *One Armed Swordsmen*, the film is filled with silly moments as the son of a slaughtered minister seeks revenge. There's a goofy fight scene with four men that has comical music playing over it. Wang Yu fights a man/woman monk. During another fight scene, Wang Yu's opponent uses a six-foot sword. The final fight scene reveals that Wang Yu actually had two arms, but only after he loses one for real.

1976 was truly the year of one armed movies, but the film that has stood the test of time is the wu xia flick *The One-Armed Boxer Vs the Flying Guillotine* (also known as *Master of the Flying Guillotine* and *One-Armed Boxer 2*). Much like its predecessor, the *One-Armed*

Boxer, the film is filled with fascinating, yet cheesy characters. The movie wastes no time setting the tone with an introduction to Fu Sheng Wu Chi. He has the kung fu sensei look—older male with a long, white beard. As if his look wasn't enough, they make him blind. Need more? His weapon of choice is the flying guillotine. American audiences often think of *The One-Armed Boxer Vs the Flying Guillotine* as the origin of the weapon, but it had appeared in numerous hit films before. However, Wang Yu's decision to arm his villain with the weapon is another step in making the film memorable. Actually, the character of Fu Sheng Wu Chi says everything we need to know about the movie; Wang Yu is throwing every wild, badass character trait he can come up with into the movie.

Fu Sheng Wu Chi is out to kill the one armed man responsible for killing two of his disciples. Of course, to keep the action going, he plans on killing every one-armed man he comes across until he finds the right one. To find the right one, he gets assistance from three fighters. Wang Yu is careful, avoiding a character cliché to be as simple as hero versus villain. Instead, he adds in a bevy of side characters that take the film to another level. The most memorable henchman is the Indian whose arms extend. When the arms come out, even when you know what's coming, the character is absurd, laughable, but undoubtedly memorable. Also assisting Fu Sheng Wu Chi is a Thai boxer and a slew of characters with interesting twists—one uses hair as a weapon, another has a comical mustache, and one has Executioners from Shaolin-style iron testicles. The villains and side characters were enough for a dozen different movies, but the movie needs a hero to take on all these odd characters.

Last, there's the One-Armed Boxer himself. Played by Jimmy Wang Yu, the One-Armed Boxer is introduced training his students. After a seemingly simple task of jumping, Wang Yu effortlessly walks upside down across the bottom of ceiling. Forget an introductory fight because this one-armed bad ass can walk upside down. Wang Yu has successfully established the villain and hero, notifying the audience up front that they are in for an absurd martial arts film.

The viewer gets unapologetic absurdity. The reality is that this film is not for everyone. Film snobs will be turned off by its high level of trashy antics. Trash film snobs may be turned off by the high level of borrowing from other classics. It's hard to fault Wang

Yu for taking his and others' best moments and throwing them into one movie. After all, the man was blacklisted from a well-known movie studio that had made him famous. In an odd way, *The One Armed Boxer Vs. The Flying Guillotine* becomes a bastardized, Tarantino-esque love letter to Jimmy Wang Yu's one-armed stardom. The film takes great moments of trashy to pretentious films and meshes them into one, action-packed script. Simply, the level of badassery is only surpassed by the infamous, off-screen Wang Yu.

Meatcleaver Massacre (1977)
by Andrew J. Rausch

The 1977 film *Meatcleaver Massacre* (also known as *Hollywood Meatcleaver Massacre*) is one of schlock cinema's best kept secrets. This low-budget shocker, produced by movie memorabilia collector Ray Atherton, is best known for its wraparound sequence featuring legendary actor Christopher Lee. Humorously, the footage of Lee had been shot for a different film and was spliced into the film during post-production.

Production executive and co-director Steve Singer approached cameraman Guerdon Trueblood, Sr. about making the film. "We're gonna make this film," Trueblood remembers Singer telling him. "He said, 'We've got this great title, and we can sell this movie to the drive-ins in Texas. They don't give a shit what the film looks like. They'll buy anything.'"

"Ray Atherton loved movies, and he had always wanted to make one," remembers Woody Wise, who appears in the film. "He made the film for very little money, and he borrowed *everything*—cameras and equipment. I don't think he spent much on the film, and I don't think anybody got paid. It was just a labor of love. We did it for fun." Wise himself wasn't an actor, but Atherton asked him if he could play a doctor. "Sure, I'll do my best," Wise said. His scenes would be filmed inside the Paramount Hospital in Paramount, California, during the day with the hospital filled with patients. "I was single at the time," Wise says, "and I ended up taking one of the patients out on a date. It was kind of fun being a movie star for a day."

The film's production was low-rent to say the least. (Trueblood believes the film's final budget was $47,000, which was quite extraordinary for a film shot on 35mm.) Much of the cast consisted of the film's crew, from cameramen to producers to grips. One such actor, who appears in a walk-on role as a reporter in a courtroom scene, is credited as "Ed Wood." The actor is shown at a distance and does not speak, making it difficult to confirm that this is indeed *the* Ed Wood, so-called "Worst Director of All Time."

Wood experts are divided on this possible appearance. *Muddled Mind: The Complete Works of Edward D. Wood, Jr.* editor David C. Hayes believes it's him. "Of course it's him," Hayes says. Wood biographer Rudolph Grey (*Nightmare of Ecstasy: The Life and Art of Edward D. Wood, Jr.*), on the other hand, says flatly, "It isn't him. It's a different Ed Wood."

So who's right?

"Ed Wood was definitely there on the set of the film," explains cameraman Roy Wagner. According to him, Wood was initially hired as a still photographer (which would explain his appearance in the film amongst all the other crewmembers). However, when the film's original director, Keith Burns, who apparently split time behind the camera with Singer, found himself unable to finish the picture, Wood stepped in and directed a number of scenes himself.

Wagner specifically remembers Wood directing two scenes in particular. The first was a scene that took place in a comedy club in North Hollywood. That scene, however, wound up on the cutting room floor. The second scene Wagner remembers Wood shooting took place on location in a house on Outpost and Cahuenga in Los Angeles.

Wagner says the shoot was poorly planned and poorly managed. According to Wagner he ultimately walked off the set, taking his camera home, after Atherton refused to pay him the $500 he was owed. "To be honest with you, I've always been surprised that an actual movie resulted from that shoot," explains camera operator Wernher Krutein. "It was just a crazy, low-budget affair."

"It was filmmaking by committee," Wagner says. "It was very bohemian. If an independent film was being made in Hollywood, all of us young filmmakers just kind of showed up and worked on it. This was no exception."

Wagner says the crew was aware of just who Wood was. "It wasn't a big deal," Wagner says. "His reputation was that he was a hack;

that he'd never made it. He was seen as a bad director. Of course, he didn't *know* he was a bad director, but that was his reputation. None of us thought anything about him being there. We all knew him. He was kind of old at the time, and he wasn't really famous or anything. It wasn't really until the Johnny Depp movie came out that he kind of gained notoriety. I kind of wish I had spent more time with him now. He didn't dress like a woman or anything like that; he just wore a white shirt and a vest. He was just one of the guys."

The film certainly looks as bad as (if not worse than) anything Wood ever directed. "The company that purchased the film [Group 1] did not pay the lab bills at Deluxe and used a work print to strike a print," Wagner explains. "That's why the film looks so bad."

Editor James Bryan, who later directed his own cult horror film, *Don't Go In the Woods*, was hired by distributor Brandon Chase to recut *Meatcleaver Massacre*. "A producer friend of Brandon's had shot the Christopher Lee material for a horror project that didn't get made. Brandon bought it for the purpose of an advertising advantage with Lee becoming his marquee name for *Meatcleaver Massacre*. We screened both films—the finished *Meatcleaver Massacre* and the reasonably generic Lee footage. We talked about a beginning, middle, and end approach to spread Lee pretty much equally through *Meatcleaver Massacre* to sell the 'starring' advertising of Lee. Brandon screened my first cut and said, 'Fine, Jim.' And so Group 1 released it nationally."

"Ray Atherton was very proud of that Christopher Lee footage," Wise recalls. "He had lost control by selling the film for $30,000, but he still wanted it to be as good as it could possibly be, and that footage gave the film a star." The integration of this footage also explains why, over the years, Christopher Lee has repeatedly said he never made a film titled *Meatcleaver Massacre*; technically he's correct.

At the end of the day, *Meatcleaver Massacre* is a fun, shoddy little film that deserves to be rediscovered and reexamined. Again, it's not good, but it deserves a place amongst similarly slapdash genre pictures as a trash cinema favorite with a cult following of its own.

Monster-a-Go-Go (1965)
by E.D. Tucker

Bad movie fans and critics alike often cite Ed Wood's legendary *Plan 9 from Outer Space* as the worst film of all time. They certainly have an argument based on writing, acting, directing, and just about every other conventional film element but one thing you can say for *Plan 9*, it was completed by the same crew that started it. In 1961, Wisconsin cult filmmaker Bill Rebane began production on a modest science fiction feature titled *Terror at Half Day*. Unfortunately, he ran out of funding somewhere around the 80-percent completed mark and filming was stopped. Four years later, another cult filmmaker, Herschell Gordon Lewis, was looking for a co-feature for his film *Moonshine Mountain* when he discovered the remains of *Terror* in a lab.

Lewis, who had served as photographer on some of this footage, proceeded to cobble together everything he could salvage and filmed only the minimum amount of new material necessary to pad it out to feature length, a mercifully brief 65 minutes. According to the ad campaign for the retitled *Monster-a-Go-Go*, "an astronaut went up—a 'guess what' came down!" and a WTF? is what we ended up with!

Underscoring the film's schizophrenic nature, the plot manages to somehow be both simplistic and convoluted at the same time. A capsule returning to Earth from a manned space flight goes off course and crash lands somewhere outside Chicago near the small town of Half Day. The astronaut pilot has become a mutated monster, apparently due to some experimental radiation protection spray, and goes on a killing spree.

To fill out the screen time between attacks, scientists wander around in the woods, experiment in their lab, and have dinner while theorizing on what might have caused the transformation. At one point in the story, one of the major characters is suddenly killed and then replaced by a similar character that is supposed to be his brother. Two months have supposedly passed during which the brother has captured the monster, experimented on him, come close to developing a cure and then had him escape. This sounds like it might actually be interesting but none of it is shown on screen, it is just discussed in dialogue between two scientists.

As you might expect from a film with a production history this unusual, what ended up on the screen is a very mixed bag. On the plus side, the stark black and white photography is very good and helps to give the film some of the '50's science fiction flavor it seems to be going for. The sound recording is perfectly fine on some scenes and almost unintelligible in others. When one actor talks to someone over the radio, the disembodied voice sounds like it was recorded with the microphone in a tin can. The acting wavers between good and absolutely awful. In one early scene when the astronaut's wife is told about her husband's disappearance, the boy playing his son stares right past the actors talking to him and speaks directly to the camera as though it was the only other thing in the room. The main cast is surprisingly competent for a film of this budget; both Peter Thompson and June Travis were established actors but seem to have ended their careers on this picture.

One of the major detractions of the film is the special effects, or lack thereof. Exactly what portion of the effects were finished is hard to say but many scenes play out with the cast describing the gruesome condition of a body laying on the ground in front of them that is nothing more than an actor making a bizarre face. Henry Hite, a seven-foot-plus tall Vaudeville performer, was hired to play the mutated astronaut and looks pretty creepy staggering around in a silver space suit. Apparently no one could decide exactly how mutated he was supposed to be from scene to scene and his crusty-faced makeup changes from mild to extreme and back again with no regard for continuity. Hiring a tall actor to play the monster was not a bad idea given the financial constraints, but apparently the prop man was not informed about the gimmick. When the crashed space capsule is discovered early on in the film, it is so small it looks like a child could barely fit inside it. This disparity was so obvious to Lewis that he played it up in the ads asking how a monster that big could fit in such a small capsule.

It is extremely difficult to judge the components of this film by the final product because there is almost no way to determine what was originally intended. The portions of *Terror at Half Day* that were completed appear to have been shot chronologically, which was a major break for Lewis, but this also meant the crucial element of an ending was missing. As it stands now, in what is possibly the most anticlimactic conclusion in film history, the monster is chased into a sewer system by a seemingly endless barrage of stock footage. As the combined forces of the military, police, fire departments and NASA scientists converge on the tunnel, all that is found is an empty space suit floating in the water. To add insult to injury, a pompous narrator then informs us that the astronaut and capsule were found landed safely on the other side of the globe and this monster probably never existed! I am willing to bet that during its limited theatrical run more than one soda, half eaten box of popcorn, and even theater seat were probably hurled at the screen at this point by angry patrons.

Night Train to Terror (1977)
by Michael Harris

Night Train to Terror is the cinematic equivalent of saying, "Screw it." This horror anthology (kind of) film is comprised of three previously unfinished films condensed into a 95 minute fun-filled delight. It is not a true anthology film like *Creepshow*, in which the segments were meant to be 25-30 minutes each and were written that way. *Night Train to Terror* takes what are presumably the best parts of these three films and places them among wraparound bits in which God and Satan discuss whether a particular character in each of the three segments deserves damnation or salvation. Before any philosophical debate begins, though, we are treated to the sounds of an on-board nameless 80s band that performs the same song four different times. It's not a bad song, and it never gets tiresome, nor does the film, despite its slapped together nature.

At first glance, one may instinctively think that all this means *Night Train to Terror* is going to be a heap of dung. Such is not the case. It's more of a heap of fun, especially if you go into it with the right mindset. I originally saw this film on a crappy quality DVD, an obvious VHS to DVD transfer. Seeing *Night Train to Terror* on Blu-Ray (yes, I saw this movie on Blu-Ray…and paid to do so) is like seeing a different movie. The image is not distorted, and the picture quality is very good. To be brief, the three stories are: 1. A man (John Phillip Law) is used as bait to lure women into an organ harvesting operation. Richard Moll from *Night Court* is in this segment as an orderly. 2. A man has an affair with another man's girlfriend and is, as a strange kind of revenge, invited to participate in a "death wish club." This is not a club that involves repeated viewings of those Charles Bronson movies. This segment features some curb-jumping style acting and an animatronic flying bug. 3. A writer's latest book makes the claim that God does not exist. This man is wearing what must surely be a toupee. Satan, or one of Satan's employees wants Bull to work for him at Satan Industries (We Put the "E" in Evil). The man who plays Satan looks like a cross between David Cassidy from *The Partridge Family* and Simon Ward, the actor who played a Satan-esque character in *Holocaust 2000*. That's pretty much all you need, but this segment also features some funny Claymation effects, Cameron Mitchell hamming it up, and disco music! The first film appears to have been made in 1982 or 1983, the second film around the same time, and the third film is definitely of 1979 vintage. If it's not obvious from the big collars and the disco music, it is from when Cameron Mitchell looks at a newspaper article from 1944 and says, "that was 35 years ago." I can do math good.

Night Train to Terror is one of those many horror/sci-fi/adventure films of the period between 1974 and 1990 which are, to some from the outside, disposable and unworthy of a second glance. I, however, embrace such films, and more often than not, am rewarded with a fun movie-watching experience. It all depends on your mindset as you go into it. If you go into such a movie thinking it will have no redeeming qualities, chances are your mind will not be changed. If you allow yourself to be immersed in a bizarre world full of oddities, you will sometimes be rewarded.

The new Vinegar Syndrome Blu-Ray release of *Night Train to Terror* contains two enjoyable commentary tracks. One track features the guys from the slasher movie podcast *The Hysteria Continues.* This track is the more informative of the two about the film. These guys have done quite a bit of research and help to unravel some of the mysteries of this film. One very interesting note is that the first segment, about the man used as bait for women to harvest their organs, was again re-edited into a film released in 1992 entitled *Marilyn Alive and Behind Bars.* The star of this segment, John Phillip Law, was brought back ten years later to shoot new scenes in this film that pretty much revolves around a different plot. The guys have lots more information to divulge and I will not repeat any of it here as it is their research, not mine, that has uncovered this information. I did suspect, though, and it is mentioned in the commentary track, that the three segments in *Night Train to Terror* were originally

Mormon movies, made to teach life lessons. It is mentioned in the commentary that the gore and nudity in the film were filmed separately from the tamer parts of these segments to make the film more marketable and to recoup some money. Not referenced in the commentary track is the connection between participants in *Night Train to Terror* and *Savage Journey*, a.k.a *Brigham*, the 1977 Mormon film about Joseph Smith and Brigham Young. In that film, Maurice Grandmaison, who appears in the third segment of *Night Train* as Pipini, plays Brigham Young and Richard Moll plays Joseph Smith. The third segment of *Night Train* (later finished and titled *Cataclysm*, and released in a Troma box set) in which they appear was made only two years later. *Cataclysm* and *Savage Journey* were both directed by Tom McGowan. John Carr directed the first and second segments.

One of the other credited directors of *Night Train to Terror*, Jay Schlossberg-Cohen, provides an interesting commentary track; however, his is more the story of his career in show business. Eventually, the topic of *Night Train* is covered, and we learn more interesting bits of information about the background of this film. Schlossberg-Cohen directed the gore and nudity portions of the film.

Night Train to Terror is a fun potpourri of strangeness, something most welcome by me. I suggest you purchase the set (it comes as a Blu-Ray/regular DVD combo pack) from the retailer of your choice, unless the retailer of your choice is a Lane Bryant or Home Depot, in which case, you may have a hard time finding it.

Nightmare at Shadow Woods (1987)
by E.D. Tucker

The 1980s were a turbulent time for American cinemas. The studio system was methodically reclaiming the movie theaters and home video was beginning to spread its blight, but there was still a little of the old grindhouse magic left. By 1987, the odds of finding a grindhouse gem at the local cinema were about as rare as finding any meat in a public school lunch hamburger. My fearless movie-going pal John Hickey and I would dutifully scour the local newspaper every Friday with the faint hope that there might be something new at the theaters besides the latest lame Michael J. Fox comedy or Patrick Swayze snooze fest. It was on one of these Fridays that my eyes fell on a newspaper advertisement for a film I had never heard of before, even in the pages of my beloved Fangoria magazine. This ad showed a fanged skull rising in the moonlight from behind a tombstone with the promise that "some things never rest in peace." Jackpot!

We walked into our home town Litchfield theater that weekend, the Cinemas West, anticipating some good old fashioned exploitation entertainment but we had no idea what we were in for. Our first clue came immediately following our ticket purchases when the theater's assistant manager, Wayne, who always looked more like a real estate agent in his ill-fitting blue blazer, appeared from out of a dark corner and greeted us with "I bet you boys are here to see the turkey of the week!" Did I mention we were on a first name basis with most of the employees at this theater due to our almost weekly pilgrimages?

Realizing that it would only add to our cinema going experience, Wayne went on to explain that we were in for a really bad one this time. According to him, we were about to see a slasher movie where the majority of the budget looked like it had been spent on the "star"—Louise Lasser from the 1970s soap drama *Mary Hartman, Mary Hartman.* Better yet, this film had been completed in 1983 and was gathering dust on the shelves when some studio needed a filler film to hold their spot at the theater when some major picture was running behind on its release date. I have no idea how he came by this information back in the dark days before the Internet, but needless to say our already bright fires of enthusiasm for this film were now firmly stoked!

Contrary to the newspaper ads, *Nightmare at Shadow Woods* is a fairly predictable slasher film firmly rooted in the 1980s vein which, by 1987, was already starting to run dry. The film begins with a flashback to a drive-in in the grand old year of 1974 where most of the patrons, including a young Ted Rami in a two-second cameo as a rest room condom salesman, are dressed more like the 1980s than the 1970s. In one of the cars, *Nightmare's* only name actress, Louise Lasser, who looks just as old here as she does in the rest of the film, is trying to make time with her boyfriend while her young twin sons are supposedly asleep in the back seat. While Mom makes out, Terry and Todd sneak off for some good-natured mischief at the passion pit. Things take a turn for the gory when Terry finds a hatchet in the back of a truck and decides to do a little chopping on a young couple doing the nasty in their car. After the girl runs naked screaming and jiggling into the night, Terry frames his shell-shocked brother for the murders and we bid 1974 farewell.

Ten years later, as the film informs us, we find Mom visiting Todd in a mental institution where he has spent the better part of his adolescence following the drive-in incident. Presumably, Terry has been normal this whole time after getting his pagan blood lust out of his system. Todd's doctor thinks he is making a breakthrough from his seemingly catatonic state and remembering the events from the night of the murder—including the fact that he didn't do it. A reunion between mother and son ends in some gratuitous pumpkin pie mashing when Mom proves her grip on reality isn't much firmer than her son's.

Later that night at dinner, we find out that 1. It's Thanksgiving, 2. Mom and her new squeeze, Brad, are getting hitched and 3. Todd has escaped from the loony bin and is most likely heading home. The combination of holiday stress and a soon to be legal rival for his mother's affections are enough to reawaken Terry's inner psycho and Todd's escape gives him just the excuse he needs to start carving up the rest of the cast like the Thanksgiving turkey. From this point forward things get pretty bloody as Todd wanders around his family's apartment complex trying to convince people he isn't committing the string of grisly murders Terry is framing him for, Mom gets progressively battier, and the psychiatrist and her assistant try to recapture their escaped patient.

After a fairly generous body count and some impressive special effects courtesy of Ed French which transcend the film's limited budget, we wrap up with a final showdown at the apartment pool between Todd, Terry, Mom, and Terry's pseudo-girlfriend Karen. Todd finally gets fed up with Terry's frame job but it's obvious self-defense isn't something they teach in mental institutions and the psycho siblings end up in the pool with Todd on the receiving end of a butt kicking. Right after Terry pulls himself out of the drink, Mom shows up packing a piece and makes darn sure this is one slasher who won't be popping back up for any last minute surprises. The film's happy ending is cut short, though, when it is revealed that Mom has gone completely around the bend and thought she shot Todd. Thankfully Louise Lasser places the gun to her head and puts the audience out of its misery after watching her histrionics for the past ninety minutes.

Time has been surprisingly kind to *Nightmare at Shadow Woods*. What once seemed like a behind-the-curve routine slasher film now stands as a time capsule of the 1980s. Whether intentional or not, this film documents everything from over sprayed hair to way too short guy shorts to the dawn of home video games and all while a maniac runs around slicing up clueless teens. We also get the typical horror film elements of over the top gore, a killer who seems to be everywhere at the same time, and the obligatory nudity compliments of a gratuitous shower scene. What we don't get, probably due to the film's early-in-the-decade origins, is the killer coming back from the dead multiple times to provide a supposedly shocking ending.

Beginning life under the title *The Complex* (as in apartment), the film then became known by the more generic moniker of *Blood*

Rage before finally seeing release as *Nightmare at Shadow Woods*. John and I thought *Turkey Terror* would have been a far more appropriate title due to the Thanksgiving setting and truth in advertising. Whatever you call it, this one week wonder was out of theaters before anyone had time to question the misleading ads. It popped up shortly thereafter on VHS from Prism Entertainment, as *Blood Rage*, in an uncut version before disappearing from video shelves about as quickly as it did from the theaters. Some fifteen plus years later, the film debuted on DVD under the *Nightmare* title in a bizarrely edited version. The gore is significantly trimmed down, the scene in the psychiatrist's office which sets the tone of the "modern" portion of the film is missing, and a new scene at the pool is added that contributes nothing to the plot.

Diehard fans of 1980s horror films are strongly encouraged to seek out the VHS *Blood Rage* version of this film until it gets a proper release on DVD and/or Blu-Ray. The combination of impressive gore and 1980s scenery make for a fun walk down memory lane and it's the perfect after Thanksgiving dinner movie to get your mind off irritating relatives. With the glut of generic product hitting the rental boxes almost daily, this film screams out for a special release. Hopefully it will be one where some of the key personnel can shed some light on its origin and troubled release history.

Plan 9 from Outer Space (1959)
by Greg Goodsell

It was my good fortune to recently view Edward D. Wood Jr.'s *Plan 9 from Outer Space* on a stadium-sized movie screen. Rifftrax, the masterminds behind TV favorite *Mystery Science Theater 3000*, were on hand to breathe life into the legendary science-fiction stinker with witty asides and snide remarks. The end result was one of unbridled hilarity, which provided comfort as this writer has always found *Plan 9* to be rather...unremittingly tragic.

Winning by a landslide in a poll conducted by Golden Turkey brothers Harry and Michael Medved as "The Worst Movie of All Time," *Plan 9* retains that title among people who haven't seen that many movies. Any seasoned movie viewer will attest to the fact that there are far worse films that don't retain the fascination of *Plan 9.*

The film's failure is directly traceable to writer-director Edward D. Wood Jr., who was in over his head on many things, in particular science-fiction. *Plan 9* appears to be Wood's attempt at recreating the thrills found in *The Day the Earth Stood Still* (1951) and *Earth Vs. the Flying Saucers* (1953). In those epics, flying saucers attack Washington D.C. or land a stone's throw away from the White House lawn. In *Plan 9*, toy-store model spaceships—and not pie tins or hubcaps as mentioned in legend—fly over a San Fernando graveyard and raise a proto-Gothic beatnik girl (Vampira) from her grave to kill two grave diggers. It's all part of "Plan 9"—plans one through eight remain a tightly guarded secret—by space aliens Eros (Dudley Manlove) and Tanna (Joanna Lee) to alert us earthlings to our wicked ways.

Banged out by Wood in his typical alcoholic haze, the movie fails to explain how humanity would be brought to its knees with the deaths of two gravediggers. One could picture how this would play out across breakfast tables across the nation:

WIFE: Hon, did you read this in the paper? A girl came back to life in a graveyard and killed two gravediggers!

HUSBAND: Well, I'll be God damned! Tell me, how did the Dodgers do?

Utilizing existing footage of Bela Lugosi for a project that was never finished, and quite a few years after his death in 1956, Wood then introduces us to the character of "the Old Man." Walking out of a pitifully plain tract home, the onetime horror great finds time to sniff a rose from a nearby bush, when our far-from humble narrator Criswell—the one guilty of saying the quote at the beginning of this article—intones this lugubrious bit of nonsense:

"The grief of his wife's death became greater and greater agony. The home they had so long shared together, became a tomb. A sweet memory of her joyous living. The sky to which she had once looked, was now only a covering for her dead body. The ever-beautiful flowers she had planted with her own hand, became nothing more than the lost roses of her cheeks. Confused by his great loss, the old man left that home, never to return again."

Bela exits stage left, we hear a car screeching, a scream—and another one bites the dust. At the old man's funeral, as the mourners leave a crypt that plainly served as a refrigerator box in a previous life, the body of the two gravediggers are discovered. Enter some cops just this side of Keystone: Inspector Clay (wrestling icon Tor Johnson), Patrolman Larry (Carl Anthony) and Lieutenant Harper (Duke Moore, who scratches his lapel constantly with his loaded gun). Johnson's Swedish accent is highly apparent. "Who found him?" "Medical, uh, examiner been 'round yet?" "Finding a mess like this oughta make anyone frightened." Wood had the foresight to make Johnson's role in *Bride of the Monster* (1955) silent, and has Johnson killed off shortly afterward by Vampira and Lugosi's stand-in, played by a chiropractor drafted into service who holds a cape in front of his face.

In the meantime, airline pilot Jeff Trent (Gregory Walcott) and his lovely wife Paula (Mona McKinnon) discuss the recent flying saucer phenomena. You would think that being an airline pilot would pay better than it does in the film; the Trents live near a graveyard and have the same exact furniture on their front porch as they do in their living room! In spite of the recent wave of reanimated corpses and flying saucers breaking out all around them, Paula insists that her pilot husband not be overly concerned about her safety. "Now, don't you worry. The saucers are up there. The graveyard is out there. But I'll be locked up safely in there."

Anyone reading this knows the story by now. There's lots of talk, stock footage, and a confrontation of members of the military and police force by the two unarmed, ineffectual aliens in their very terrestrial spacecraft. The recent shabby activity, Eros claims, is because the human race is on the verge of creating the much dreaded "Solaranite bomb." Say what?

"Take a can of your gasoline. Say this can of gasoline is the sun," Eros passionately explains. "Now, you spread a thin line of it to a ball, representing the Earth. Now, the gasoline represents the sunlight, the sun particles. Here we saturate the ball with the gasoline, the sunlight. Then we put a flame to the ball. The flame will speedily travel around the earth, back along the line of gasoline to the can, or the sun itself. It will explode this source and spread to every place that gasoline, our sunlight, touches. Explode the sunlight here, gentlemen, you explode the universe. Explode the sunlight here and a chain reaction will occur direct to the sun itself and to all the planets that sunlight touches, to every planet in the universe. This is why you must be stopped. This is why any means must be used to stop you. In a friendly manner or as (it seems) you want it."

According to legend, this bit of pseudo-science about Solaranite was the script addition of Wood's long-suffering wife, Kathy Wood, who lived to the ripe old age of eighty-four. Standing by Ed through thick and thin, as the 1994 Tim Burton biopic *Ed Wood* dutifully mentions, Kathy never remarried after Wood's death in 1978. It was my good fortune to see Kathy at a film convention with other members of Wood's repertory at a Hollywood film convention in 2000. I figure that Ed was drawn to this small, feisty woman due to their shared fondness for drink. It appeared that Kathy had a snootful that morning and told the assembled audience that her Eddie had "a wonderful life!"

Back to the movie: Things deteriorate, the stupid, stupid earthlings get into a tussle with Eros, and the wobbly spacecraft takes to the skies where it catches fire and explodes like a firecracker. So much for superior alien technology. Criswell reappears to ask, "Can you prove it didn't happen?"

We could go on all day about *Plan 9*. The mere appearance of John "Bunny" Breckenridge as the alien ruler seemingly exists only to topple Zsa Zsa Gabor's claim as *The Queen from Outer Space* (1958). The spaceship interior consisting of radio equipment, old and outdated by the time the film was made, on wooden tables. Furiously scribbled dialogue that strives for importance but all too surely shows sign of alcohol-fueled dementia. It's all been cited and enjoyed numerous times before, so we won't go there.

What is it that makes *Plan 9* a dispiriting experience for this writer? Blame falls solely to the participation of Jeron King Criswell of "Criswell Predicts" infamy. Serving as a narrator to an already off-the-rails narrative, Criswell's booming voice intrudes on the stoic non-action to either state the obvious or attempt to wax eloquent over Wood's turgid, purple prose.

A radio announcer, Criswell is said to have reportedly made a few off-the-cuff predictions one day when he was short on news copy. Some of the predictions actually came true and, smelling money, Criswell donned a tuxedo and a newfound mysterious persona. Becoming a fixture on Johnny Carson's *Tonight Show* for several years, Criswell went on to publish several books based upon his highly unreliable predictions. Among his many unrealized prophecies was that his good personal friend Mae West would be elected president of the United States in 1960 and that he and West, along with his other personal friend Liberace, would fly to the moon five years later!

While a cheerful fraud in private, confessing that he couldn't tell anyone what the weather was like staring out of a window, Criswell's participation is what makes *Plan 9* for this writer a gloomy experience. Criswell calls to mind the lonely, paranoid homeless person on the street corner, his flight-of-ideas delivery a classic example of dime-store schizophrenia. Criswell can be a funny guy, until you are regularly confronted by people just like him, who insist that fluoridation is a communist conspiracy to sterilize the western world, or that there was more than one gunman on that grassy knoll, or how vaccinating your children makes them autistic.

It's been said that when *Plan 9 from Outer Space* is screened, the world is automatically transported to a place where the time is perpetually three o'clock in the morning, with long, dark shadows. The tragedy surrounding its makers permeates every frame and again the disembodied head of Criswell reappears to ask us, "Can you prove it didn't happen?"

Well…can we?

Planet of the Vampires (1965)
by Andrew J. Rausch

There are many great horror movies out there that you simply don't know about. Sure, everyone is familiar with *A Nightmare on Elm Street, Friday the 13th, The Blair Witch Project,* and the like, but what about the movies that might not have been as big of a commercial success but should still be considered some of the genre's finest work? I'm excited to tell you about one of my favorite "lost gems" of all time: the egregiously underrated *Planet of the Vampires.*

At first glance, *Planet of the Vampires* could easily be mistaken for just another kitschy 1960s sci-fi B-movie. But those in the know revere this movie as one of the first crossover horror/sci-fi films, a front-runner for great movies like *Alien* and *Event Horizon.* Filmed at Cinecittà Studios in Rome, the movie features an international cast and was shot by director Mario Bava on a shoestring budget—but Bava did such a great job of making the film look like a big production that you definitely wouldn't think otherwise while watching it.

In the film, two large interplanetary exploration ships, the *Argos* and the *Galliott,* respond to a distress signal originating from the unexplored planet Aura. Upon their attempts to land, both crews become possessed by an unknown force and violently try to kill each other. Only through the willpower and efforts of Captain Mark Markay, commander of the *Argos,* is the *Argos's* crew prevented from seriously injuring each other. Upon traversing the treacherous molten terrain of the planet to reach the now-unresponsive *Galliott, Argos's* crew discovers that their comrades on the other ship were not as fortunate as they were; they lay strewn about the ship, apparently murdered by one another.

The unknown forces that originally possessed the *Argos*'s crew return, but instead of occupying the living survivors, the forces inhabit the bodies of the dead crew members, reanimating them from their hastily-constructed graves. While fending off the reanimated creatures and trying to fix the *Argos* so they can escape, Markay and the survivors come across a crashed alien ship housing huge skeletal remains of other aliens. The crew knows their situation is dire, and they are in a race against the clock to escape the force that has inhabited the bodies of their dead comrades. In a thrilling climax, much is revealed about the true nature of the unknown force, and the movie boasts not one but two inspired plot twists at the conclusion of the film that even I didn't see coming!

The creation of the film itself has some amazing stories as well. The production was so pressed for time, the actors—who came from a variety of international backgrounds—all spoke their lines in their native languages (including English, Portuguese, Italian, and Spanish), often times having no idea what the other actors were saying. This helps to explain the nagging sensation the viewer will encounter when it seems that some actors' lines are dubbed into English, causing a disconnect between the actors' mouth movements and what they are heard to be saying, while others appear in perfect synchronization.

Since the film was so groundbreaking for its time, the studio really had no idea what to name it. The original Italian title of the film, *Terrore Nello Spazio*, translates to *Terror in Space*; other titles attached to the movie in its various stages of pre- and post-production included *Planet of Blood, Space Mutants, The Demon Planet, The Haunted Planet, The Outlawed Planet, The Planet of Terror,* and *The Planet of the Damned.* The indecision in naming the movie most likely came from the fact that the type of creatures portrayed in the film— reanimated humans possessed by an unknown force—had really never been clearly defined before this movie was released. Even though the film's title is *Planet of the Vampires*, the beings portrayed here are actually closer to zombies, but this film was released in 1965, three years before George Romero's *Night of the Living Dead* would adequately characterize this genre for us.

As previously mentioned, the film was shot working under a very minimalistic budget. It already looked remarkable (for its time), but Bava's finished product is even more impressive with this knowledge. Extensive use of miniatures and forced perspectives are used in the film, including tons of colored fog on the planet's surface to help hide the fact that they were actually just shooting on a bare-bones set. In an interview with Tim Lucas, Bava expounded on the process: "Do you know what that unknown planet was made of? A couple of plastic rocks—yes, *two*: one and one!—left over from a mythological movie made at Cinecittà! To assist the illusion, I filled the set with smoke." According to Lucas, the two plastic rocks were multiplied in several shots by mirrors and multiple exposures.

One scene that Bava didn't want to skimp on, however, was the sequence where Markay and two other crew members encounter a derelict alien spaceship. As the astronauts clamber around the large ship, they discover multiple skeletal remains of gigantic, long-dead alien life forms. This scene draws immediate comparisons to the extended "space jockey" scene in Ridley Scott's film *Alien*, and rightfully so; produced fourteen years after *Planet of the Vampires*, Scott's scene has a great deal of similarity to and evokes much of the same feel as the one presented in this movie. Upon *Alien's* release in 1979, the horror magazine *Cinefantastique* ran an article pointing out not only this obvious similarity, but other minor parallels between the two films. Both director Scott and screenwriter Dan O'Bannon claimed at the time that they had never seen *Planet of the Vampires*.

Even without all of this fun background knowledge of the movie, *Planet of the Vampires* is an incredibly rich story and a great viewing experience that has withstood the test of time and can easily entertain the true horror fan of today. I highly recommend you seek this movie out and give it a watch. You won't be disappointed.

The Prowler (1981)
by David C. Hayes

I have to tell you that I love the slasher sub-genre of horror films. I cut my teeth on them as a wee lad and have appreciated the minimalist effectiveness of the good ones. I've also lamented to the heavens about the bad ones. Through the years, beginning around 1978, the slasher took off and began to set box office records. Classics like *Halloween, The Texas Chainsaw Massacre, Friday the 13th*, and *My Bloody Valentine* set the stage for a horror boom market that had a pretty good run. The slasher film quickly became derivative and a mockery of itself as the "group of teens in danger from a psychotic mass murderer" formula began to play itself out. The mid-1990s saw a resurgence in the slasher film, most notably from Wes Craven's *Scream*, that saw the sub-genre become self-referential, almost a meta-film wherein the audience and the filmmakers were fully aware of the cliché. The 1990s also presented the world with prosumer home video equipment, and that, my dear friends, is where the biggest issue lies. The slasher film, because of its budget-friendly nature, was the genre of choice for backyard hacks with a video camera and some dopey friends. This, more so than the original surge of product in the 1980s, has given the slasher film a bad reputation. It is good, though, to remember our roots and take a peek behind the shower curtain before it was homogenized, bleached, and put out in mass market rip offs, one after the other.

The Prowler, directed by genre-veteran Joseph Zito (*Bloodrage*) in 1981, is an example of someone doing something a little different from the "damsel in distress" formula and turning it into a surprisingly effective thriller. Unlike the bastard children of the modern era, Zito and his crew had to be competent filmmakers. Remember, this was

1981, so there were no videotapes, power cords, and work lights. Films were, well, they were films, as in shot on film. Not only was this expensive, but using 35mm film was difficult and only trained technicians were capable of it. Lighting needed to be used effectively, and it was much more of a process than turning on some headlights. All in all, in order to make even a bad film in the 1980s, one had to be a competent technician. That competence shines throughout *The Prowler*. Thanks to a beautiful print and the diligence the archivists show to its genre releases, it is easy to see the subtleties involved in what is, truly, a very gory film. Tom Savini has called *The Prowler* some of his best work, and I would have to agree. Pitchfork slayings—in the shower no less—bayonets, etc. New viewers of this film will no doubt be impressed with the ingenuity of death involved.

The Prowler is a little more than that, though. As I alluded to earlier, the story itself is very interesting. Beginning in 1945, at the close of World War II, we find out that a woman named Rosemary has, cryptically, written a Dear John letter to her fiancé who was in the European theater. The war ends, the boys come home, and at the Avalon Bay Graduation Dance, a young couple is slaughtered by a prowler in a Nazi soldier's fatigues. Flash forward to 1980 and Avalon Bay is having its first graduation dance in thirty-five years…cue the bloodbath.

What *The Prowler* really owes its look and feel to are the Italian giallo films from just a few years prior. The work of Bava and Argento in crafting the use of a killer's point of view and the seemingly random (until the dealer of death's motivations are explained in the final reel) victim selection are really the pre-cursor to the slasher of the early 1980s. More importantly, the look of *The Prowler* can be traced to the black gloved, leather-clad, devious antagonists of *The Bird with the Crystal Plumage* (1970), *The Bay of Blood* (1971) and many more. Where the language barrier may have been preventing the giallo films from taking off in the states (or, more likely, the horrible dubbing), *The Prowler* and its brethren featured good old American hack actors and not imports.

That really isn't fair. Sorry, Mr. Zito. A surprisingly good cast rounds out the production. Farley Granger, Vicky Dawson, and Christopher Goutman turn out fine performances and we are reminded, again, that the lack of opportunities for actors in general meant that, even in the slasher flicks, the cast could be first rate.

It is a shame that *The Prowler* hasn't really been recognized for the quality production it is. Films that followed owe it a great deal, whether or not anyone realizes it.

Revenge of the Virgins (1959)
by Jan Pippins

Take a wussy tenderfoot with gold fever, his ball-busting wife, a stereotypical old drunken prospector, desperados, army deserters and the worst rubber rattlesnake ever. Splice in post-production scenes of topless "Indian maidens" (a hook for audiences in the days when low-budget films weren't censored). Welcome to 1959's *Revenge of the Virgins*.

Without the nubile natives, *Revenge of the Virgins* was an uninspired drive-in Western about ill-fated Anglo treasure hunters out to steal sacred gold. With the added topless Indians, it became something else. Directed and produced by Peter Perry, Jr. (famous for 1961's *Honeymoon of Terror*, 1978's *Cycle Vixens* and other sexploitation softcores), it was the first nudie Western and, more recently, a source of disagreement among cult cinema connoisseurs.

Revenge of the Virgins begins with documentary-style footage featuring the last all-female tribe of bewigged, topless Native Americans in California. Whether creeping listlessly through wilderness or dancing like sloths on Quaaludes, they're accompanied by Kenne Duncan's plummy narration. A B-movie actor, Duncan was a pal of schlockmeister Edward D. Wood, Jr. and appeared in several of Wood's flicks. His voiceover is a truncated, inaccurate history of California tribes that warns against "the savage guardians of the Golden Horde." Cue dramatic music foreshadowing Something Important about to happen. Cue faux Indian drums.

One member of the cast, the actor billed as Hank Delgado, says, "I remember very little about making the movie. It didn't take very long, maybe a couple of days. There were a number of us from the Pasadena Playhouse who were in it—Charles Veltman, Jr., Jodean

Russo [Lawrence], Lou Massad, Ralph Cookson. We thought it was a just the standard 'B' Western. We were just happy to be in a movie and to be paid. We weren't paid much, but the checks cleared and it didn't always happen that way." It was his first movie and first Western. "I had a prominent part and I just acted my brains out." Proud of his work, he included the movie on an early resume. Then a friend told him about the topless sequences. "Oh, my god! I did not want to be known for *that* kind of movie, so off the resume it came!" Who could have guessed it would be a cult favorite decades later? Not Delgado.

The movie he thought he was in begins when greenhorn Melvin Potter (Charles Veltman, Jr.) hears grizzled prospector Pan Taggart (Stanton "Stan" Pritchard) boast of gold in the creek bed of the aptly named Gold Creek. Taggart claims he would be a rich man except for the deadly tribe of Indians who defend the gold. Thanks to introductory sequences, viewers know this is an all-female topless tribe, but Taggart doesn't mention that. If he had, maybe the bartender (Ralph Cookson) and his customers would have paid more attention to the old prospector's stories. Instead, everyone ignores Taggart except Potter. The tinhorn is dazzled. His avaricious wife Ruby (Jodean Russo) dreams of saloon ownership, but Potter uses their gin-mill money to finance a Taggart-led hunt for the gold. Soon the Potters ride for them thar hills with the old prospector and two gunslingers, Wade Condon (Hank Delgado) and Mike Horton (Hugo Stanger). The gunmen intend to steal Potter's money, the gold, or anything else of value.

As the journey continues, the fortune hunters feel eyes on them and worry about Apaches. Since they're in California, it seems geography was nobody's forte. Meanwhile, sequences of the nudie cutie tribe demonstrate that someone is watching but it ain't Geronimo. According to the website d2rights.blogspot.com, the five supporting "virgins" were unsuccessful strippers or models. The exception was Nona Carver as the stone-faced leader of the faux natives, a golden-haired white woman considered a goddess by the others. Carver was a well-known stripper, Kenne Duncan's girlfriend and later played the madam in Ed Wood's lost 1970 softcore comedy *Take It Out in Trade*. Sporting bows, arrows and perky boobs, the tribe stalks increasingly restive gold-seekers. Ruby ("Shut up and get back to work!") becomes even more unhappy with her hapless hubby. Meanwhile, Condon lusts for fetching, bitchy Ruby and the gold. His partner Horton just wants the gold. He's eager to plant Ruby six feet under, but she dodges death when Army deserters Jones (Louis Massad) and Curt (Del Monroe) show up. Jones and Curt have overheard talk of the gold and are determined to join up.

Condon protests, but is overridden by Ruby. Frightened by Taggart's tales of bloodthirsty Apaches, she persuades the others that Jones and Curt will help protect them. Miffed, Condon and Horton ride ahead ostensibly to scout, but intending to ambush and kill the deserters. Instead, Mike Horton gets an arrow in the back.

Next to die is young deserter Curt. At the creek, an arrow drops old Pan Taggart when he stands up and shouts that he's found gold. Not to be discouraged by the rising body count or sounds of Indians chanting in the distance, the group stays put. They find a whole heap of nuggets before an arrow kills Jones and one of the nubile natives stabs Ruby.

Survivors Wade Condon and Melvin Potter both want all the gold and it's clear they're not destined to be BFFs when Condon plugs Potter in the back, grabs the gold and attempts to skedaddle. Lucky for Potter, the bullet struck a gold coin in the lining of his vest. Instead of dying, he shoots Condon, who unfortunately isn't wearing any magic bullet-deflecting coins.

But Potter isn't on a winning streak and upon hearing tribal chanting off camera, grows nervous. Blinded by fear, he doesn't see the venomous rubber rattler nearby. Suspended on unseen strings, it bobs like the flying saucer in Ed Wood's *Plan 9 from Outer Space,* then flies at Potter and attacks him. Falling to the ground, Potter is set upon by "the savage guardians of the Golden Horde" who drag him off, presumably to his death.

As credits roll, it's easy to see why *Revenge of the Virgins* has been called a classic of sexploitation, a cheapo grindhouse rip-off of *The Treasure of the Sierra Madre,* simply bizarre and the worst movie ever made. However, anyone asserting the latter apparently didn't see *Glen or Glenda?* (1953) or *Plan 9 from Outer Space* (1959), two spectacularly awful offerings from Ed Wood.

But was *Revenge of the Virgins* also one of Wood's strange jewels? Cult cinema aficionados disagree. Dead 2 Rights blogger Joe Blevins maintains the Woodsian touches made a believer out of him—*Virgins* screenwriter Pete LaRoche was none other than Wood. "Ed had different fake names for different kinds of assignments. Pete LaRoche seemed to be one he used exclusively for his Western work." Robert Craig includes *Revenge of the Virgins* in Wood's filmography in his book *Ed Wood, Mad Genius: A Critical Study of the Films*, but Wikipedia leaves it out as does the website "The Hunt for Ed Wood," although the site admits that considering the evidence, LaRoche might be Wood.

As for the rest of the cast and crew, some became very well-known. Latvian-born cinematographer Vilis Lapenieks (1931-1987) survived the lousy camerawork in *Revenge of the Virgins* to carve out a lengthy film and TV career. Jodean Russo became Jodean Lawrence and worked extensively on stage, in film and TV until her death at age seventy-seven in 2010. Hugo Stanger (1901-1990) acted in TV and films for three decades. The late Del Monroe may be best remembered for playing Seaman Kowalski in *Voyage to the Bottom of the Sea* (both film and TV series), but he was a working actor until 2005. Louis Massad acted on a number of TV series in the 1960s and 1970s.

"I seem to remember that Lou wanted to try producing and I think Ralph Cookson quit acting and became a cop," says the former Hank Delgado. He changed his name to Henry Darrow and never stopped acting his brains out, shooting to international fame as Manolito Montoya on the classic Western TV series *The High Chaparral* (1967-1971). During a remarkable stage and screen career lasting over half a century, Darrow has been a trailblazer for Latinos in the entertainment business. He has garnered numerous awards including an Emmy and an ALMA for Lifetime Achievement. His favorite actor is versatile megastar Johnny Depp, who played the title role in the 1994 Tim Burton bioflick *Ed Wood*.

Riki-O: The Story of Ricky (1991)
by Shannon L. Grisso

Prison has provided the backdrop for many of the most enduring images and moments throughout cinema's illustrious history. Something of a genre all to itself, the prison film has provided some all-time classics, films that come up fairly regularly on "Best Of" or "Classic Movie" lists. Whether a statement on the resilience of the human spirit (*The Shawshank Redemption*), the detailed examination and recreation of a daring escape attempt (*Papillon, Escape from Alcatraz*), a hard-hitting expose on the harsh realities of institutionalized life (1983's *Bad Boys, Brubaker, I Am a Fugitive from a Chain Gang*), or a character study of an individualistic rebel whom even prison cannot truly contain (*Cool Hand Luke, Birdman of Alcatraz*), the prison remains a wellspring of cinematic gems, largely due, perhaps, to the rather blunt metaphor it serves for the cages and restraints society tends to place around true rebels.

Still, every time I study a list of "all time greatest prison movies" I can't help but feel that something's missing. Don't get me wrong— *The Shawshank Redemption* really is a great movie, but I feel it really needs a scene where one character punches completely into, and through, the midsection of another character, unleashing a torrent of blood and guts. And, okay, there's that great, truly iconic shot of Tim Robbins, arms to the side in a pseudo-crucifixion pose, but at no point does he take the opportunity to drive home the emotional intensity inherent in such a pose by shouting "*Bastards!*" at the top of his (hilariously dubbed) lungs.

And okay, I'll admit—the characters played by Dustin Hoffman and Steve McQueen really do establish and share a deep and enduring bond on their common "need to be truly free," but nowhere in the revered *Papillon* do they express this bond by one teaching the other how to take a simple leaf or blade of grass, and blow on it to produce a flute solo that outshines any of Zamfir's pan flute pieces. Nowhere.

And, yeah, I get it—in most of these movies, the warden stands as the ultimate symbol of oppression. In fact, if you prefer, in most movies the chief warden is pretty much a dick, a total control freak who delights in taking the very last shreds of our hero's humanity. But in none of the often cited prison classics do you have a warden who actually becomes a monster, an eight-foot-tall, rubbery-looking beast with a bad habit of just letting snot trail right out of his nose in large, ropy streams.

Another staple of the prison movie is to establish sympathy and understanding for our characters by showing us their backstory. Usually it's a relatively petty crime that accidentally gets out of hand (Sean Penn's vehicular manslaughter, which lands him in the reformatory, is really just an accident, for example), or maybe a set up or coincidence that leads to unjust imprisonment (as in what basically ends up happening to Tim Robbins in the beginning of *Shawshank*), but there's only one movie I know of where the hero comes to prison with five bullets lodged inside his chest, "souvenirs," he claims, fired at him by the bastard he blames for killing his girlfriend.

And yeah, yeah, yeah, I know—our hero in all these movies has to undertake some pretty drastic measures to prove himself in the eyes of his prison peers, such as when Sean Penn improvises a pillow case full of soda cans in *Bad Boys*, or when Paul Newman refuses to throw in the towel when getting beaten to a pulp by George Kennedy in *Cool Hand Luke*. So how come none of these movies on those typical "Top Prison Movies" lists don't include a scene where our hero gets ground up glass shreds thrown directly into his eyes and his right arm badly hacked open during a fight scene, leading to our hero's awesome comeback: first he bursts open a water main to wash the glass out of his eyes, then he reaches into his badly-slashed arm and takes the two severed ends of one of the major veins and ties them together, while—in the meantime—he has rather nonchalantly used his other arm to pop his opponent's eyeball right out of his head?

In fact, I can think of only one prison movie where all that awesome crap happens, although, to be honest, that's just for starters. In addition to all that amazing stuff, our hero also gets a huge spike shoved in one hand, which just causes him to punch his attacker with his other hand (and his punch literally causes his attacker to explode). In another showdown our hero lands a series of three punches on a much larger opponent. The first punch makes the opponent's arm burst open at the elbow; the second from the knuckles to the wrist. Not to mention, this film is the only I can think of, prison genre or not, which actually utilizes a large, industrial-strength meat grinder to its full potential (that of grinding up the body of the warden in his monster form, spraying blood *everywhere*). It's the only film in which a dog gets kicked in half, a character gets forced to swallow a handful of razor blades (which he then spits into the face of his attacker), the head of an extra is crushed between the fists of one of the bad guys (in a shot utilized on TV's *The Daily Show*, at one point), and our hero punches into and through numerous villains, even punching the top half of one character's head entirely off.

The one prison movie I'm thinking of is the gloriously, ludicrously over-the-top spectacle known as *Riki-Oh: The Story of Ricky*, a truly gonzo 1991 Hong Kong production derived from the late 1980s Japanese manga. *The Shawshank Redemption, Midnight Express, Escape from Alcatraz*, etc. are all great movies, they really are, but they're pretty heavy going, and to be honest, I'm not always in the mood to watch something that serious. *Story of Ricky*, on the other hand, is one of those rare movies I'm always ready to watch, so for that reason alone, I think it belongs not only on every "Top Prison Movie" list, but it belongs right on the top of each said list.

All my life I've had this unshakeable fear of having to go to prison. It's not that I live a law-breaking life—truth be told, I behave myself pretty well, down to the point of being quite boring, actually—but more because I know if I ever did end up in prison, I'd be in some serious trouble. I'm not a very streetwise person, so the cons and scam artists would certainly make short work of me; I'm a short, skinny little wuss whom the bullies could abuse and amuse themselves with at their will; and, while certainly no heartthrob material, I do think my sweet ass would probably swap for lots and lots of packs of cigarettes, if you know what I mean.

Hopefully I'll never find out for sure, but if things do happen to go bad for me and I do wind up tormented and abused in some institution somewhere, then maybe, just maybe, I'll hear this haunting flute music, and I'll turn around and there I'll see Ricky, ready to lend a helping (and invincible) hand. I know we'd never be able to bond with him teaching me his techniques (his superhuman strength seems to derive, somehow, from very carefully-controlled breathing, which my asthma would prevent; likewise, the asthma would also prevent me from perfecting the leaf/grass blade flute symphony technique), but that's okay. I'd be more than content to just sit back and watch ol' Ricky go to work!

One last note—it's not a movie, but the TV show *Oz* could also have benefited from Ricky's presence. This show, which ran for six full seasons, would have probably lasted about six minutes before Ricky would have burst those walls down!

Next time you're in the mood for a great prison flick, but none of the classics seem to have the blood, insane violence, bizarre set pieces, and just sheer over-the-top "what the hell is going on?" atmosphere, trust me. Give *Story of Ricky* a chance. You'll be glad you did.

Robo Vampire (1988)
by Shannon L. Grisso

The two greatest questions you should ever have to answer about any movie you've seen are "Was it any good?" and "What's that one about?" They are simple, direct questions that anyone can answer, whether a pretentious, artsy-fartsy film buff or just a casual movie-goer. Every once in a while, though, you watch a movie so strange, so indefinable, so one-of-a-kind, that these two questions become much more difficult to answer.

Case in point: the 1988 Hong Kong/Philippines co-production entitled *Robo Vampire*. At least, I think it's a Hong Kong/Philippines production. The credits list one "Joe Livingstone" as director, but most online sources credit legendary quickie kung-fu king Godfrey Ho as the real perpetrator.

But okay—we don't care about the credits; we only care about those two questions, so here goes.

"Hey, Shannon, is *Robo Vampire* any good?"

Hmm…like I said, this is a very tough question. Turns out *Robo Vampire* is one of those movies where terms like "good" or "bad" just don't apply. So I'll have to come back to that one.

"Hey, Shannon, what's *Robo Vampire* about?"

Okay, that one really should be easy; I'll just describe the plot.

Robo Vampire concerns the struggle between a drug dealer (who looks a little like Sonny Bono) and the anti-drug agents out to stop him. Sonny Bono's drug shipments keep getting intercepted by these drug agents, so he decides to employ vampires to help protect his drugs. You'd think this would be no big deal—the agents could just move in when the sun was out, and the vampires would be powerless, right? Well, not so fast…see, Sonny Bono doesn't use regular old vampires, he uses hopping vampires!

(The hopping vampire, for those unfamiliar, is a regular fixture in many Hong Kong horror movies. These vampires attack by holding both arms straight out in front of them, and can move only by hopping short distances. To get them to stop advancing and attacking, you have to take a piece of sacred parchment and stick it on their foreheads. Like my wife pointed out, all you really need is a good supply of Post-It Notes and you're safe.)

Anyway, a weird magician/wizard type named Tomas (I think) is responsible for training and activating the hopping vampires. As he is working one night, Christine, a ghost/witch type in a see-through outfit, attacks him out of the blue. Turns out he turned her lover, Peter, into one of those hopping vampires. While they fight, magician Tomas activates another vampire, who, for some strange reason, is also a gorilla. Turns out that this hopping vampire gorilla is actually Christine's lover, Peter!

We also have the drug agents, who intercept Sonny Bono's next shipment. They are unprepared for the hopping vampires, though, and lose this battle. One agent gets his face burned off by hot steam from one of the hopping vampires; another is actually blown up when Gorilla Vampire Peter shoots sparklers out of his sleeves at him.

Still with me?

Okay. Next, a couple of scientists operate on one of the two drug agents, who, it turns out, is barely alive. They decide to use his body to make an "android-like robot," which seems a little redundant to me, but hey, I ain't no scientist. And these guys must be scientists—they have this cool lab with all these machines with big, sparkling lights. There's one awesome machine that has a big red minus symbol on one side and a big green plus symbol on the other (See? Total scientists), and they build the robot with a hollow metal torso and road flare.

The robot's armor consists of what looks like oven mitts spray-painted silver. Actually, the armor really may be oven mitts, because it sure isn't very protective—on his second mission, he gets hit with a bazooka blast and is totally blown to hell! The scientists aren't too worried about this development; they say, "Emergency! Save the robot at once!" I found this very optimistic, as it didn't look like there was enough of the robot to bother saving, but, again, maybe that's why they're scientists and I'm not. This time they use an even bigger, brighter road flare to fix him, I guess because he was so badly damaged.

Other than his lame-ass armor, I guess he's an okay robot. He has a cool, reverberating robot voice, and even grunts and groans all robot-like during some of the fights, and any time he turns, swivels, takes a step, or makes any movement at all, you hear a cool whirring sound.

So, basically, what you have here is a series of showdowns between the drug agents (with their new secret weapon, the "Robot Warrior") and Sonny Bono's drug runners, interjected with a subplot about ghost/witch Christine and her star-crossed lover, Gorilla Vampire Peter. In between escalating showdowns and developments in these main storylines, we do have a few other interesting bits.

There's a great scene where Chief Thompson (the head of all drug agents, I think) assigns Ray to help save their two undercover agents, who have been discovered by the drug runners. Ray asks what the assignment is worth, and the Chief says, "I pay one million, but the government only pays twenty grand." Ray, whose mercenary skills are definitely better than his negotiating skills, demands thirty grand. Personally I think he should have gone much higher; Chief Thompson and he could have met in the middle somewhere, but hey, maybe that's why I'm not a mercenary either.

Another priceless bit of dialogue comes when some of Sonny Bono's thugs are causing trouble in a small village. They mess with a couple of guys enjoying drinks at a roadside stand, and when one of the two guys defies their bullying, the bad guy says, "Who are you?"

"We're two of the meanest fuckers around, that's who!" is the immortal reply. It's too bad this film is so obscure, because this exchange demands to be on one of those "Top 100 Movie Lines of All Time" posters you see every so often.

You know what? The more I try to describe this movie, the more confusing it sounds. And in a way that's accurate—this is a damned confusing movie, after all—but truth of the matter is I'm just over-thinking this whole thing, just like some pretentious, artsy-fartsy film critic would.

So let's do this again:

"Hey, Shannon, is *Robo Vampire* any good?"

Yes, yes, oh God yes. It's great, in fact.

"Hey, Shannon, what's *Robo Vampire* about?"

It's about the best, most delirious, bizarre, and entertaining ninety-one minutes you could spend in front of your TV screen.

In fact, if I were a scientist, I'd take my cool machine with the red minus symbol and the green plus sign, and give this one a definite green plus!

Robot Monster (1953)
by Tony Schaab

In the 1950s, a classic era of film reared its head within the science fiction genre. Now, yes, some of the movies made in this time were hokey, utilizing poor special effects and sometimes even worse acting, but there were others that rose to the top. The original *War of the Worlds* and *Forbidden Planet*, both made in the '50s, are some prime examples of great films of the era. On the other end of the spectrum lies the dirty, gritty, and sometimes campy primordial ooze of science fiction B-movies.

This is where you'll find *Robot Monster*.

The story in a nutshell: a young boy named Johnny falls and is knocked unconscious. When he awakens, he finds that an alien, Ro-Man, has invaded the Earth and killed all of humanity except for eight people (random, right? Oh, those quirky aliens and their plans…). Conveniently, the survivors are Johnny's family and a few scientists.

The character of Ro-Man, one of the most popular 1950s-era movie monsters, is played quite obviously by a man in a huge gorilla suit with—get this—a diving helmet on his head which has a TV antenna attached to it. The ridiculous costume was only one of many unintentionally hilarious moments in this film. Using a few thrown-together pieces of what looked like old radio equipment, a dresser with tape over the mirror, and a bubble machine, Ro-Man was able to communicate with his superior.

The survivors are immune to Ro-Man's "Calcinator" due to Johnny's father injecting them with his newly discovered antibiotic. Fending off Ro-Man's ability to locate them with a not-so-technologically-advanced series of wires strung around the perimeter of their shelter, they await a couple of scientists who are traveling to reach an orbiting space station which houses soldiers who will save the day; that is, until Ro-Man foils their plans. In one particularly bad scene, you are actually able to see the hand and arm of a member of the film crew holding the space ship that carries the two scientists.

But back to the story: after killing two of the remaining survivors, Ro-Man finds himself attracted to the pretty twenty-something daughter. In a somewhat disturbing scene, he captures her and takes her back to his cave, where he tries to molest her. Ro-Man is ordered by his superior to kill the remaining humans, including the girl; however, the monster finds that he just can't find it in his heart to follow through with the order.

For a few glances at some noteworthy lines, there's a funny scene in which Ro-Man rationalizes the dilemma between his feelings and his commands, and he laments "at what point on the graph do 'must' and 'cannot' meet?" A personal favorite was when Johnny tells Ro-Man that he looks like a "pooped-out pinwheel."

One of the most memorable features in this movie was the re-use of footage from older movies. Specifically, *Robot Monster* features a clip of an alligator (with a fin attached to its back) and a monitor lizard wrestling each other (from 1940's *One Million B.C.*), along with a borrowed stop-motion dinosaur from 1925's *Lost World*. These "lifts" understandably provided comic relief for some viewers and confusion for others.

As one might expect, there are many inconsistencies in this movie, including when Johnny falls at the mouth of the cave when Ro-Man makes his entrance. In his initial fall, Johnny is wearing pants, yet he wakes up with shorts on. There were also scenes re-used in different parts of the film, likely due to a strained total budget of $16,000. The movie was filmed over the course of only four days; originally released in 3-D, it astoundingly grossed over $1 million. The director, Phil Tucker, was only twenty-five when he made *Robot Monster*.

At the time of the movie's release, some reviewers made a connection between Ro-Man and the Russians. Filmed during the Cold War era, it must have been obvious that all Americans believed the Russians were going to invade, kill them, and rape their women. The phrases "Ro-Man" and "Russian" were even directly mentioned in some reviews as sounding awfully similar.

Bad acting, bad effects, and an absurd creature costume all combine to make this a ridiculous spectacle of a movie. From the inconsistencies to the random vintage dinosaur footage, the film turns into a farce. If Tucker had found more money to bring in the robot he originally wanted instead of the haphazard ape suit, I have to wonder: would the film have been better? If this had happened, however, we would have been deprived of the vision that is Ro-Man in all his strange glory. If you really believe in aliens, and furthermore are ready to accept that they look like a rejected *Spongebob Squarepants* villain, then you'll likely feel right at home watching this movie.

Aliens invading with the objective of eliminating the human race is not a new concept, but this particular story does have its unique elements. Throughout the course of the film, we find that the aliens are unable to kill this family due to some sort of super antibiotic they have taken; yet, at the end of the day, the humans were still more than vulnerable to physical attacks, no matter how feebly they are doled out. There are a few additional twists and shocks in the death scenes, but overall the story is fairly weak and smells of desperation.

Of course, this wouldn't be a Grade-A example of a campy B-movie if the inconsistencies weren't plentiful. It was obvious that Tucker filmed some scenes with the express purpose of being reused over and over again. Ro-Man and his superior are one and the same, but their repetitious and blundering movements stand out. If your spaceships have visible fishing line attached to them, that's one thing, but when a whole arm can be seen, that's too much. Tucker seemed to have trouble finding enough footage to fill the measly one hour run time, so he reverted to splicing in the above mentioned footage from other movies.

Through all of this, though, I actually do recommend that you check out *Robot Monster*, if you haven't already. This film is referenced so much in pop culture, and can be found in many places in the entertainment world, so watch it for the sake of saying you have and to get a small piece of the 1950s sci-fi B-flick lodged in your brain. It's a cult classic, after all. Just beware of enjoying it too much and being at risk of your brain freezing up, Hu-Man!

Scream Blacula Scream (1973)
by Ben Ohmart

The only difference between a good movie and a bad movie is if you like it. Camp, schlock, tat, indie, dated, whatever you want to call the greatness that is *Scream Blacula Scream*, it's just a wrong label. Stylish, daring, trying to do something different, interesting is how I tag this one. It verges right on the border between comedy and drama and I've got no idea where to put my hands in case it falls.

William Marshall is The Man. The Reason. William Marshall is the Presence that carries you from casual fan to Fan of this movie. Hell, when he looks right at you after his first meal before the credits roll, you just want to get out of there. He's looking right at *you*, honky! Run away like a girl!

"Hey, blood." It's really Marshall's voice that's the true, hands down star of this film. His majesty and deep diaphragm seem to pull from the very soles of his feet and gathers more Thurl Ranvenscroft all the way up through his throat. Kenneth Branagh and Laurence Olivier and you and me and Morgan Freeman and Leonard Nimoy all wish we had *his* voice. It was one of the great voiceboxes of cinema. (And wouldn't *Star Wars* have been a different film if Lucas had been a smarter caster?) And, alas, his voice is sadly underused here, yes....

Perhaps *Scream Blacula Scream* is not as good as the original *Blacula*. But there are a couple of things for me personally that give this sequel an edge over the first flick.

First of all, my friend Bill (son of Harpo) Marx wrote the score to this. I love Bill. When we visited him in Palm Springs, he let me wear Harpo's original wig and coat.

Yes.

And we sat by the harp-shaped pool and spoke of Marxism and pigs (his wife Barbara collects pig-shaped things) and his audio book and we even lightly touched upon *Scream Blacula Scream*, for which he has a soft spot.

Then there's a second reason. Barbara Rhoades, in all her glory. I first saw her in Columbo, then even more of her in an *Ellery Queen* episode. I could look at her easily for ninety minutes at a time. And though *Scream* doesn't showcase her great wit and full acting ability, she's a red-haired beauty (whom I wish would write a book about someday) whose hair gets bigger the more undead she is.

Then there's that Blacula cape.

Then there's that great scene when the good Count is walking down the street for the first time and, like Crocodile Dundee, he's not trying to blend in with the modern townsfolk.

There's that jive pimp Willis, in his red pool table skin hat. There's the turning into a bat effect, a dead cousin to *Abbott and Costello Meet Frankenstein*. And I'm sorry, but I watch *The Hobbit* and *Percy Jackson* and I don't see any better cartoon movement in those than in my man Blacula. They all move like cartoons. But at least 1973 didn't have the bloated budgets that keep ticket prices high now.

Ah, the 1970s. When there was true integration in the entertainment world. *Sanford and Son* as a sitcom or unscripted shaky camera show today? No. Is the afro more comical than actually shaving one's head completely? Sorry, but spend some time thinking on it. Don't just automatically go for the most familiar.

Now, I realize *Scream Blacula Scream* is a cheap, i.e. inexpensive, movie that's little more than a house party—and a series stopper (there's no *Blacula 3* out there). But what we've got here is a horror movie. Lots of walking camera, back when the walking camera meant P.O.V., not "I'm too cheap to set up the shot, besides no one complains." And it's a bit slow (if you're a fan of three-second shots, thanks to today's rash of editors). But it reeks of black atmosphere. It's a mystery and a horror movie, and it's got a scene showing four silent police cars cruising up to Blacula's house at night; no sirens, no lights. What other film dares to pay for the cop cars and then saves their batteries like that?

The vampire Blacula sucks throats and collects up vamp slaves that move like zombies, and they are totally intimidated by him.

He's even got voodoo beauty Pam Grier under his powah. Who would not be charmed, fascinated, and afraid of this dark Dracula if he was suddenly there before you, sprouting hair through his cheek lines and changing his hairline and bushing up his eyebrows when he's out for blood? Smacking whitey cops up and down, tossing them out glass windows...the man's a monster!

I wrote a book called *The Rerun of Dracula*, a comedy about Vlad the Impaler, the inspiration behind Stoker's Dracula. Vlad "comes back," having never really left, because he's tired and old and bored. Bored with life, tired of being ignored. He can't be killed, so he might as well go for the recognition. So he sues Universal, Random House, Fox, etc. collectively for his image rights. It's a comedy of copyright; since he didn't die, there's no "author's life plus seventy-five years" clause, is there? Well, I dedicated the book to Lance Henriksen, since William Marshall is no longer with us to put real regal justice to the role.

All I ask, Limited Hollywood Imagination, is that when you get around to rebooting *Blacula* (as you will), please take a little time over it and don't make it camp, as you like to do with take-the-name-and-the-idea-only remakes. Don't put a comedian in the lead, and try to give it a little grandeur like the original attempted. I know it's easier to make fun of something that came before your time than to do a proper job, but financially think about this: comedies don't win awards or make huge piles of cash (generally) like the action and drama flicks do, because no two people agree on what's funny. So, play it straight for a change. Because you can't make *Scream Blacula Scream* into a PG Pixar film, can you?

Sex Kittens Go to College (1960)
by Richard Koper

From all of producer Albert Zugsmith's *High School* and *College* movies, *Sex Kittens* is absolutely his weirdest production. Zugsmith (1910-1993) produced several movies for Universal Studios in the mid fifties. He worked with director Jack Arnold on the classic *The Incredible Shrinking Man* (1957) and with acclaimed directors Douglas Sirk—*Written on the Wind* (1956) and *The Tarnished Angels* (1957)—and Orson Welles, *Touch of Evil* (1958), before he decided to take the directorial task upon himself. His first outings were both released by Universal International.

College Confidential and *The Private Lives of Adam and Eve* (both released in 1960) starred Mamie Van Doren, who would also star in *Sex Kittens. Adam and Eve* ran into problems with the Catholic Legion of Decency. They tried to ban the movie and crusaded against Zugsmith and the actors in it. Because of this, Universal Studios ended the association with Zugsmith.

Meanwhile the filming of *Sex Kittens* had commenced in December 1959. After completion, Zugsmith had a hard time getting it released. When the movie premiered on August 24, 1960, its audience mainly consisted of teenagers. A movie theater owner in Harrisville, Michigan, noted that "eighteen walked out the first hour, all teenagers, and five of them asked for their money back," while an entrepreneur in Ellsworth, Kansas, commented that he "used [the movie] for late show on Saturday night for the teenagers. They loved it!"

Van Doren graduated from a (twenty-eight year old!) student in *College Confidential* to the (twenty-eight year old!) head of the Science Department in *Sex Kittens Go to College*. "You are a bit much for a growing boy to face at nine a.m. every morning," Mamie is told when assigned to teach at Collins College.

Van Doren plays Dr. Matilda West, who has an IQ of 298, speaks eighteen languages and holds thirteen University degrees. But the main reason she was selected by the computerized robot THINKO must have been her vital statistics. "40-20-32, and a blonde," clumsy lab assistant Etta exclaims. But Public Relations Director Barton reassures the College professors: "You can't blame THINKO. How can a machine know we wouldn't like someone who looks like Mamie Van Doren."

Dr. Zorch finds it hard to believe that THINKO has come up with this over-classified woman to head his department and hastens himself to the train platform where the all-girl College brass band awaits the arrival of Miss West.

Legs Raffertino and hoodlum pal Boomie travel on the same train as Dr. West. The two heavies want to confront 'Sam' THINKO about the betting it has been indulging in. They assume for unknown reasons that the Science department of Collins College is actually a cover-up for a bookie racket.

When Boomie identifies Dr. West as a striptease dancer called Tassels Montclair a.k.a The Tallahassee Tassel Tosser, she decides to be honest about her past: "If I've got the name, I might as well play the game." On an evening out at the local nightclub, The Passion Pit, Mamie hypnotizes her colleagues Zorch, Watts and Towers. She lets them make fools of themselves, when they follow her every move in a bump and grind show number called "Baby Daddy-O."

At the end of the film Dr. West tells Barton: "I must accept myself as I am." She decides to go back to burlesque. Luckily she is saved from this downfall by Barton who asks her to marry him. While Matilda West downplays her sexpot image, professor Carter and Etta Toodie have turned into tight clothed blondes themselves. I guess in the fifties a curvy blonde couldn't be a genius. Van Doren makes it clear that all women are seductive sexpots at heart.

The usual mix ups and misunderstandings stand for the comic situations in this movie. Maybe the ambiguous dialogue was daring for its time; now it's quite corny. While dancing the Charleston, Mamie asks John Carradine how he feels about oral examinations, "Do you find them exciting?" To which he answers that he goes to the dentist twice a year.

Another suggestive piece of interaction is witnessed in a scene with Tuesday Weld and Norman Grabowski. Jody (a not so dumb blonde) is madly in love with moronic football team captain Woo Woo, who has an inferiority complex. Being worked on by the gorgeous Jody, he exclaims: "You know I don't kiss girls!" To Miss Weld's disappointment, he only thinks of her as a pal. "It's a crying shame you're not a boy. Just to think of all the good times we would have together." He makes it even worse when he tells the confused Judy: "Ma says I was slow developing. They called me peewee until I was fourteen. And then all of a sudden... 'Woo Woo'!"

In the end Woo Woo is cured from his latent homosexuality. Through his sleepwalking and the explanation of his dreams in psychoanalysis with Dr. West, Woo Woo has found his true libido. "You do better asleep than most men do awake," Dr. West tells him. To which an excited Jody adds: "A hundred thousand dollars better!"

The working title *Sexpot Goes to College* excluded Van Doren as the only sex-driven girl on campus, but the new title includes junior sexpot Tuesday Weld and foreign exchange student Mijanou Bardot. Yes, she is the (less glamorous) sister of French sex kitten Brigitte. As Suzanne, Bardot overacts as the stereotyped nymphomaniac French girl, who flirts with every man in sight. She studies "The American Male," and to gangster Legs Raffertino she says: "I write big book," glancing down on him, "Oooh, very big book...on how American men make love."

Because of a brawl between the professors and the gangsters, THINKO is having a nervous breakdown. We see the robot stuttering Aahs and Oohs, while smoke is all around him. Is he having a mechanical orgasm?!

Matilda West asks him what kind of dreams he is having lately, while a nurse—*Playboy* centerfold and Marilyn Monroe look-a-like Arline Hunter—is holding THINKO's hand. The vision blurs and when the sight clears we see THINKO and Dr. West's assistant Voltaire, a chimpanzee, in the empty Passion Pit drinking bourbon.

A cleaning woman comes in and starts to strip! A second stripper performs her act for THINKO, lying on the floor in only her panties. And if that wasn't enough to stimulate the teenage boys in the audience, a third dancer starts to disrobe in front of the monkey and the robot. She bumps and grinds and works THINKO's groin by humping on him. Finally a beautiful brunette dances seductively before THINKO while Voltaire plays the piano with his feet.

After almost ten minutes we get the message of what THINKO and every red-blooded male in the audience is dreaming about!

Louis Nye played Dr. Zorch. Zorch's assistant is played by Maila Nurmi, better known as her alter ego Vampira. She had just appeared in Ed Wood's shlock classic *Plan 9 from Outer Space* (1959). After her part in *Sex Kittens* she was out of work and found herself "house-cleaning for friends, charging 99 cents an hour." Her clients included *Sex Kittens* co-star Tuesday Weld, Troy Donahue, and Tab Hunter.

Former child actor Jackie Coogan became a star in Charles Chaplin's *The Kid* (1921) and decades later played Uncle Fester in TV's *The Addams Family.* Charles Chaplin's son played a small part, as did Harold Lloyd's son. Chaplin Jr. died at the young age of forty-two from a blood clot. Harold Lloyd Jr. was a troubled soul, a closeted homosexual and alcoholic, who died of complications from a stroke when he was only thirty-four years old.

Pamela Mason was actor James Mason's wife. Cult actor John Carradine appeared in more than 300 movies, including the Z-grade *Revenge of the Zombies* (1943), *The Unearthly* (1957) and *Hillbillys in a Haunted House* (1967).

Besides this incredible cast, the absurdity of the plot, the trivial dialogue and the added strip scenes make watching this movie a fun experience. Well, at least for those who can bear stereotyped views on women, homophobia and corny adolescent jokes for more than an hour and a half.

Silent Night, Deadly Night Part 2 (1987)
by David C. Hayes

Good or bad, the intention of a sequel, at least in the horror genre, is to expand on the themes and storyline of the original film. We've seen it done well, like *Aliens,* and we've seen it done poorly, like *Return of the Living Dead: Rave to the Grave.* Although grave raving may be the new "it" thing, one cannot imagine that the themes of the original are being represented in this sequel. Regardless, each of these films took the original idea and brought it to a different world on a grander scale. Look at the original *Leprechaun,* for example. Five films later and we're in space. Not good, but bigger. That is the entire point. This is how sequels have worked ever since the concept was invented (with 1933's *The Son of Kong*). This doesn't apply, apparently, to Christmas slasher films. Many people love the original *Silent Night, Deadly Night* from 1984. It's cheesy and dopey but the film had guts. Many people didn't enjoy the film so much and found that protesting its very existence was a good enough life goal.

Some of them, like Lee Harry, liked the original so much he took a bunch of footage from the original, cut out the gore, added the brother of the original killer in a "grown up" psychiatric interview and released it as *Silent Night, Deadly Night Part 2.* It's like the Dreidel Song, second verse same as the first.

This is no joke. The sequel is, for all intents and purposes, the original film all over again. Not a re-imagining or an *Evil Dead 2-*style improvement, it is actually the original footage. I know that the VHS business was cut-throat and wacky in the 1980s, but when would this ever be a good idea? If you've seen the first film, you know that a boy sees his parents murdered (and mother raped) by a drunken Santa Claus. He and his brother grow up in an orphanage with a very strict Mother Superior and the boy, Billy, gets in all kinds of trouble. He eventually grows up and gets a job in a toy store during Christmas. Smart move, right? The toy store Santa calls in wasted and Billy is forced to put on the suit, resulting in a killing spree of jolly proportions. Billy is put down in front of his little brother Ricky and the day is saved. Years later, Ricky (this is where the *Part 2* starts) is being interviewed by a psychiatrist. He describes all the awful things Mother Superior did to the boys. We see these as well but don't worry, you won't have to remember anything new because it is the exact same footage from *Part 1*. Ricky then describes the awful things that Billy did as Santa Claus...and again we are treated to *Part 1* with a Ricky voice over. Ricky finishes his story and we're about forty-five minutes, well over halfway, into *Part 2*. The remainder of the film is Ricky chasing a now wheelchair-bound Mother Superior around the orphanage looking for vengeance. Yay. It's not good, but at least it's new. To be fair, the new footage with Ricky's killing spree is freaking hilarious. Ricky, played by the completely over-the-top Eric Freeman, has these bizarre eyebrows that flip and dance and undulate when he gets angry or kills people. These eyebrows, quite effectively, steal the show.

But that brings us to the quandary. The sequel is supposed to fortify the themes of the original film. The themes of the original film were, by all accounts, a narrative based on creating a holiday horror film that would, until the end of time, be dusted off year after year and enjoy a new round of revenue and create new fans as a morbid "holiday tradition" was passed from generation to generation. Lee Harry, Eric Freeman and those goddamned eyebrows derailed that for a good many years. Not only did Part 2 not keep the theme alive, it inspired even more insipid sequels.

There were a few other sequels, going up to number five, for the *Silent Night, Deadly Night* series and, thankfully, they did not continue the re-hashing trend. If they did, though, *Part 3* could be one of the other orphan kids telling a psychiatrist about Ricky's interview which tells about the events of the first film. This could go on forever like one of those picture-in-a-mirror-in-a-mirror pictures. If that were the case, I would break the mirror into shards and go Oedipus on my own eyes just to make it stop right around *Silent Night, Deadly Night Part 9*.

In all reality, though, the eyebrows and other, odd assorted issues with *Part 2* did not bring the *Silent Night, Deadly Night* franchise to a halt. The final film in the series, 1991's *Silent Night, Deadly Night V: The Toymaker* starring Mickey Rooney (yes, Andy Hardy himself) and written/produced by Brian Yuzna, rounded out the originals.

In the annals of film history, there is only one other holiday film that has a chance of being more inane and obnoxious than the gyrating, mistletoe-like eyebrows on Eric Freeman. Once again, when faced with what appears to be an abysmal failure in art, taste and aesthetic I go to the one man that can make any film look better: Hulk Hogan.

I still don't know how someone thought this was a good idea. There had to have been an investor to put up the millions of dollars that it took to make this. There then had to be a writer to buy into the idea. A director would then sign on. Finally, this movie signed itself a star. A great big star. A star whose light burned so brightly that not even blind people are safe from this film. Of course, I'm speaking of the former WWF World Heavyweight Champion, slammer of giants, father of the incomparably untalented Brooke Hogan and facilitator of underage drunk driving accidents. That's right, folks, the producers of *Santa With Muscles* got themselves a real live superstar. The orange golem himself, Hulk Hogan.

If *Santa With Muscles* (1996) can't fire up the warm glow of holiday cheer in your heart, then you are most assuredly human. *Santa With Muscles* makes *Silent Night, Deadly Night Part 2* look like *Apocalypse Now*, so if I leave out a few nuances and ignore the layers and layers of metaphorical relevance please forgive me. All right…an evil corporate dude with huge muscles who likes to hunt runs from the police, gets amnesia and wakes up in a mall dressed as Santa Claus. The dude then assumes he is the real Santa Claus and goes on a crusade to help an orphanage (featuring a very young Mila Kunis in her second film role) aided by Garrett Morris, who, in all fairness, was probably happy for the paycheck at this point. The orphanage is threatened by evil scientist Ed Begley, Jr. and Santa goes slapstick Rambo on the evil organization saving the kids. Santa Clod eventually comes out of the amnesia (and I wish it was communicable) and the children all end up living with him in his mansion…'cause he's rich.

There are so many places to place the blame for this flick. Watching it is the visual equivalent of tasting fruitcake and I point the finger at the big orange golem. The big guy has a penchant for taking a good idea, injecting it with steroids, and dropping the big leg on it. For example (and this is the short list): *Thunder in Paradise, Mr. Nanny, Secret Agent Club, Suburban Commando*, the final years of World Championship Wrestling…the list is endless.

Sleepaway Camp 2: Unhappy Campers (1988)
by Michael Harris

In the world of "film as art" it is not a popular notion to comment positively about a slasher/dead teenager movie, especially a sequel to a slasher/dead teenager movie. Gene Siskel and Roger Ebert coined the term "dead teenager movie" back in the early 1980s when a myriad of *Friday the 13th* and *Halloween* clones were being produced, so, it being a perfect term for these films, I have adopted the name.

The first *Sleepaway Camp* movie succeeded in creating a bizarre world for us to enter, one that, despite being about the forty-sixth film up to that point in 1983 that had been set at a summer camp, still managed to entertain thanks mostly to the casting of Felissa Rose as the quiet and shy Angela, but also thanks to the probably unintentionally strange pacing of the film. It felt like a gen-u-wine low-budget horror film and it worked very well.

I was not expecting much from the 1988 sequel, *Sleepaway Camp 2: Unhappy Campers*, by then somewhere around the 195th film to be set at a summer camp. However, I was pleasantly surprised by this film, directed by Michael A. Simpson. Pamela Springsteen, sister of Bruce and now a still photographer, does a great job of playing an older version of Angela, a version that has undergone the necessary amount of therapy to be allowed to be a counselor at a camp, a camp that is only sixty-five miles from the one at which Angela completed her handiwork in the first film. Yes, that's right, this is a silly horror film, but, like the first film, for a silly horror film it works nicely. Pamela Springsteen is great as the insane Angela who, despite belting out a lovely song about how fun camp can be and her overwhelmingly chipper nature, is quite obviously disturbed.

Angela is not pleased to know that some of the campers at Camp Rolling Hills are engaging in such things as sex. From the first film, we have learned things about Angela that I will not reveal here as some readers may not have yet seen the first film. Angela is more than a throwaway slasher film character with no personality. As played in the first film by Felissa Rose and in the second film by Pamela Springsteen, Angela is brought to life and is an interesting character to watch. As far as a connection of the character from the first to the second film, it works quite well. I could believe that the Angela from the second film was the same person as the Angela from the first film. This is a notable achievement as, if the character in the second film had seemed distant from that of the first film, it would have taken away quite a bit from the dramatic and suspenseful tension. Yes, I just wrote "dramatic and suspenseful tension" in regards to this film. I'm not changing it.

Sleepaway Camp 2 makes an attempt to incorporate a sense of humor into the proceedings and succeeds occasionally in that regard. My guess is that *Sleepaway Camp 2* is funnier than *Meatballs Part 3*, but I have not seen that entry in the *Meatballs* saga. If you have been lucky enough to see *Meatballs 4*, you may have been pleased to find that it stars Jack Nance, the lead actor from David Lynch's *Eraserhead* and Sarah "Ursa" Douglas, but it also starred Corey Feldman. No film can be perfect.

In the same way, kind of, *Sleepaway Camp 2* is not perfect. Luckily, Corey Feldman is not in it, but it does get very close to reaching slasher movie perfection, which is a different kind of perfection from regular film perfection. You always know what to expect in a slasher film. There will be deaths, mayhem, 27-year-old actors playing teenagers having sex, blood, and, if you are lucky, some pretty bad music. If a slasher film offers something extra, then, in my mind it is better than average. The performance of Pamela Springsteen as Angela and most of the performances of the supporting cast rises above what one may expect from low-budget slasher movie acting.

Even though we know Angela is several cashews shy of a full can, I enjoyed every time she was on camera. I usually find it difficult to navigate my way through a conversation that includes my attempt to defend slasher films of the 1980s. I am a fan of several of these films including *Final Exam, Silent Scream, Halloween 2* and *3, The Pit,*

The Unseen, and the aforementioned *Sleepaway Camp*. At the same time, I would be perfectly willing to engage you in a conversation about the films of Pier Paolo Pasolini, Woody Allen, Werner Herzog, and Stanley Kubrick. My love of movies is not limited to one or two genres, but just about all genres. I'm not a big fan of the rom-com, but I do not discount the idea that, over the years, there have been some good ones made, such as the wonderful *The Goodbye Girl, When Harry Met Sally*, and *Groundhog Day*.

Like its predecessor, *Sleepaway Camp 2* was very good for what it set out to accomplish. It's not Fellini or Bergman, but it kept me entertained. I think that accepting what you are heading into is important in whether or not you will enjoy a film. If you expect a slasher film from the 1980s to be more than a slasher film from the 1980s, you will likely be disappointed and offended by the kills in the film. If your mindset is such that you know what you are getting yourself into and you end up getting more for your time than a fill-in-the-blank script, you have won. I feel my time with Angela in *Sleepaway Camp 2* was successful and I am looking forward to watching the third film in the series, though, I do not know if lightning can strike twice or if the campfire will burn out, so...

Director Simpson mentions in the commentary track for the film that he would not have had any interest in this project if it had been a straight-forward horror film. The humor in the script by Fritz Gordon compelled him to have more of an interest in taking on the directing reins. Like *Friday the 13th Part 6, Sleepaway Camp 2* very much benefits from attempts to include gags throughout the film, not all of which work, but enough do to keep the film from becoming a groanfest. The humor in the film allows it not to take itself too seriously and to revel in the otherworldly silliness that these kinds of films inhabit. Slasher films are just as "out there" as science fiction films or fantasy films.

Yeah, I know. They involve death and gore, but no film is perfect. One either accepts the nature of horror films or does not. There is not much way around that fact. As someone who enjoys a good horror/slasher film from time to time, I can endorse the above average *Sleepaway Camp 2* as a film that tries hard and most of the time succeeds in being entertaining thanks mostly to its strong performances and brisk pacing.

Sorceress (1981)
by Andrew J. Rausch

Some films, such as *Citizen Kane*, gain reputations over time and ultimately become labeled as one of the finest films ever produced. Other films, like the Roger Corman-produced *Sorceress*, gain a different sort of reputation over time, ultimately becoming labeled as one of the worst films ever made. The schlocky sword-and-sorcery epic has gained a reputation as being one of the cheesiest things Corman ever produced, and even made an appearance in the 2004 documentary *The 50 Worst Films Ever Made*. And now it's coming not only to DVD for the first time, but getting its own Blu-ray release from Shout! Factory.

I had never seen *Sorceress* before and wondered what all the fuss was about. Could it really be as bad as they say it is? Was this really a must-see for the *Mystery Science Theater 3000* crowd? After all, it certainly had its B-movie credentials with Corman as producer, Jim Wynorski as screenwriter, and Jack Hill as director. (Although the fact that a pseudonym was slapped on as director is certainly reason to wonder going in.)

I sat down and talked to Wynorski to find out what *Sorceress*'s screenwriter had to say about this most infamous of projects. "I know the movie has a bit of a reputation," Wynorski says, "but I also think it has a unique charm to it—a sort of childlike innocence that you don't see very often."

So I watched the film and I have to say I agree with Wynorski's assessment. The film isn't great by any stretch—certainly not the epic production Corman might have hoped for—but it is fun in a "what will they do next?" sort of way. To get a good idea of what this movie is, you have to look at the story of its production, which is almost as interesting as the movie itself. (The making of the film is discussed on the Blu-ray's extra features interviews at great length; their often *Rashomon*-like contradictory nature makes them all the more fascinating to watch.)

In the early 1980s, Wynorski worked for Corman's New World Pictures. On the Monday following *Conan the Barbarian*'s big theatrical opening, Corman called Wynorski into his office. "He said, 'We missed the boat, Jim,'" Wynorski recalls. "He said, 'We should have had something like *Conan*...We should have beat them to it. We missed the boat.'" So Corman being Corman, he looked at the young screenwriter and filmmaker and said, "I'd like you to go and write a screenplay for a *Conan*-like project and have it back to me by next Monday." Wynorski, happy to have an opportunity and a credit, went and wrote the script in seven days.

In true Corman fashion, the film would be titled *Sorceress*—even though there isn't a sorceress anywhere to be found in the film.

Corman then hired Jack Hill, who had previously directed such noted films as *Spider-Baby* and *Coffy*, to rewrite the screenplay and direct the film. Wynorski says when he went in to meet with Hill, the director told him he had just become involved in a new religion, and that he planned to write it into *Sorceress* extensively. "I thought, 'He's the director, he knows what he's doing,'" Wynorski recalls. "So I just thought, 'Sure.'" Now fast forward to the film's first screening, and Corman discovers that his *Conan* exploitation film is filled to the brim with religious ballet dance sequences and now clocks in at more than two hours.

"Roger was really mad," Wynorski recalls. "He just stood up in the middle of the screening and went to his office. He called for Jack Hill to join him." The two then clashed over the film, and ultimately wound up parting ways as a result. Jack Hill's name would then be taken off and replaced with the name "Brian Stuart," which was a combination of Corman's sons' names.

Needless to say, the religious ballet numbers were excised from the film and the running time dropped significantly. Then several scenes got unintentional laughs at a second screening and even more footage was cut from the film. Corman then shot an additional fifteen minutes of footage (in a single day) to bring the running time back up to feature-length.

In true Roger Corman fashion, the low-budget movie impresario had several scenes shot specifically for the film's trailer. These scenes were later edited into the film by second unit director John Carl Buechler.

The resulting film is a huge mess of a movie (that made a fortune at the box office) that's a blast to watch. Filled with stilted dialogue, horrendous acting, and a number of scenes featuring bare breasts (this is, after all, a Corman exploitation film), *Sorceress* is a hell of a lot of fun. Credit both Wynorski and Hill for adding in scenes of comedic dialogue, as well, which compensate for the fact that they didn't have the budget of a *Conan the Barbarian.*

If you like movies that are so bad that they're good, or if you're just a huge B-movie fan, you're sure to find plenty to enjoy here from this good-natured little film. The Blu-ray transfer looks great, to boot. This is definitely a must-watch for movie geeks of all ages.

The Star Wars Holiday Special (1977)
by David C. Hayes

Last night I was visited by three ghosts. The first was the Ghost of Jedi Past, and he showed me the glory of the original *Star Wars* trilogy, and I marveled, like in my youth, to the adventures of Luke and Leia and that weird incestuous thing they had going on. Then, merely an hour later, I was visited by the Ghost of Jedi Present, and he showed me the horrible, computer-generated filth that passed for films as George Lucas perverted his legacy, ably aided by Jake Lloyd, with the "new" trilogy. As I lay awake in bed, shuddering from fright with the voice of Jar Jar shrilly echoing in my head, another ghost entered my bed chamber. Hunkering beneath the covers, only peeking out of cat-killing curiosity, I noticed that this ghost was smaller than the rest. And it limped. This ghost also had a hunchback and a wheezing cough that punctuated each step. Unafraid of this new ghost, I threw off my blanket and confronted it. This…thing announced itself to be The Ghost of Jedi A Little After Past. I laughed, mocking it and calling it Quasi-Ghosto. As the developmentally challenged little thing grabbed my hand, though, my laughter turned into a scream. You see, gentle reader, this malformed, raised in a basement, step-child of a ghost was taking me on the scariest adventure yet. It took me to *The Star Wars Holiday Special*.

If you are not familiar with *The Star Wars Holiday Special*, you should feel lucky. When people talk about not being able to take their eyes off of a horrendous car wreck, they are talking about this film. Originally broadcast once in 1978, and never again, *TSWHS* is a case study on why drugs should never, ever be allowed on a film set. It is also a case study on why Bea Arthur should never sing, why English is so very important to the American television viewer, and why Wookie porn never caught on.

At this point, I suppose I should tell you what the film was about. I'll do my best, because I'm not really sure. This is 1978, remember, so everything on television was a variety show. Here goes: On the Wookie home planet of Kashyyk, Chewbacca's wife, Mala, is making food for the big Wookie holiday known as Life Day. Chewie's kid, Numbnuts (at least that's what I'm calling him) is introduced as well as Chewie's dad, Grumpnuts (again, my name). All of them speak in Wook-ese to each other, and we don't have the first bits of English until Harvey Korman is on a cooking show. If you don't know who Harvey Korman is, then you are young and happy. Back to our story. The Empire is on the planet and Darth Vader (using clips from *A New Hope*) orders Stormtroopers to check R2-D2 to ask about Han's whereabouts. He doesn't know, but says they left a little while ago. Harvey Korman, in a dual role, gives up the location of Chewie's home, but he is out, so the Stormtroopers confront his family. Numbnuts runs upstairs, Mala is in a panic, and Grumpnuts does something weird. Han and Chewie arrive and throw the Stormtrooper to the ground, killing him. Han leaves. So far, we are four members of the original cast in, and they all look stoned out of their gourds! Grumpnuts watches disco legend Diahann Caroll sing in some sort of fetish, Wookie porno. We cut to the cantina in Tatooine that is being run by Bea Arthur (of *Golden Girls* fame). She sings a tune to the Cantina Music, I retch, and we're back with the furry *Brady Bunch*.

Now, if you're suffered this long through the film, you will be rewarded with…the first appearance of Boba Fett (before the re-issue debacle in 1997)! Numbnuts watches a pretty cool animated film with Luke, Han, and Boba. End cool stuff interlude.

I don't think I can get through the rest of this. In summation, Jefferson Starship and a mini-holographic acrobat troop perform, the Wookies get their Life Day celebration featuring all of our cast (the aforementioned Luke, Han, Chewie, and Leia now). Best of all…*best of all*…Carrie Fisher takes the main theme music of *A New Hope* and sings to it. Some douchetard wrote lyrics to the music about the Wookie Life Day, and Carrie Fisher, as Princess Leia, sings it to close the show. She warbles away like she is on the tail end of a three-day coke bender, and it ends. Thankfully, it ends.

Rumor has it that George Lucas is pretty upset, still, about this little fiasco. Good, he deserves it. I'm still pretty upset about *Phantom Menace*, but you don't see me throwing a hissy fit. May *The Star Wars Holiday Special* be with you, Georgie, like herpes.

Street Trash (1987)
by Bryan Shuessler

What defines director James Michael Muro's 1987 hilarious cult-horror film *Street Trash* as a "trash film"? As defined by the Webster Dictionary, trash is, "...[T]hings that are no longer useful or wanted and that have been thrown away; something that is very low in quality."

When approached by the editor of this book, Andrew J. Rausch, and asked if I would like to contribute a piece on "trash film," no sooner had I been asked which film I would like to write about, than the answer exploded within my head with more certainty and visceral clarity than anything had ever before in my life: the 1987 cult classic *Street Trash*. A film that started out as a 10-minute student film from J. Michael Muro, with a cast of no-namers (at the time of filming), it has certainly stood the test of time for this movie freak. With its motley cast of extremely memorable characters and surprisingly original storyline about a bunch of bums and vagrant street kids living on the grounds of a junkyard, this film surprisingly has not lost any of its remarkably sleazy charm twenty-seven years later. The junkyard is run by a crazy, tyrannical Vietnam vet named Bronson (Vic Noto), who rules the scrap metal graveyard with an iron fist, while the other hand is quick to wield a large knife fashioned out of human bone (possibly the femur) and ready to stab anyone showing disobedience at will. This film holds a very tender spot within my heart.

To me, the film is the true definition of "trash," even going so far as to present the word in its title. The film, written by Roy Frumkes, a director, writer, and professor at the School of Visual Arts in New York City (as well as a longtime member of the National Board of

Review), is filled with his unique blend of tasteless humor and extremely politically incorrect style of raunch and sleaze. In this viewer's mind, this completely eclipses Frumkes's work on the 1985 documentary *Document of the Dead*, which was critically-acclaimed within certain horror circles.

Street Trash has withstood the test of time, remaining a very popular and engaging piece of enjoyable filth primarily due to the depth and detail of its characters—characters that broke the mainstream barriers of decency. Consider the highly infamous and notorious scene in which a hobo in the junkyard has his penis removed after taking a leak on the always-enraged Bronson, resulting in the rest of the junkyard inhabitants engaging in a playful game of "cock keep-away." Then there's the slightly disturbing and morally perverted scene in which young, smart-ass Fred (newbie Mike Lackey) finds local hood and gangster Nick Durand's drunk girlfriend puking her brains out (which isn't much) along the alleyway of his restaurant. Quickly turning horny and wanting some dick, Fred is mistaken for her regular hot beef injection. The scene results in a dark act of rape and murder. While one watches her, kicking and screaming for help, being dragged from the tire enclave and to her venereal disease gang-bang, only to receive an even more sexually perverse desecration, a recurring thought rings out: Why is this filth so entertaining?

Both scenes depict some very real and very vile aspects of human nature, portraying multiple forms of rape—a drunk girl taken advantage of and raped only to then be gang-raped by even more scum and eventually killed in the process, followed up by some postmortem coitus by Frank (R.L. Ryan), the junkyard owner and operator. This portrayal of deviant sexual nature and lust stands out following one very dark scene and turn of events.

A playful and seemingly light-hearted game of genital keep-away is begun, superbly filmed with some very cheery music accompanying it. One cannot help but laugh, even when taking in the severity of the situation at hand. It is scenes such as this that give the film its warped humor, charm, and enjoyment. Viewers can't help but remember such a film, for better or worse, and this is just one component within the film that makes it a cut above the rest of the films considered trash films and cult favorites.

Another aspect to *Street Trash* that gives it an unfair advantage over most other films is the technical aptitude that soon-to-be-famous camera and steadicam operator James Muro, a.k.a. J. Michael Muro (credited as Jim Muro in *Street Trash*), possesses. *Street Trash* is shot and photographed beautifully. Where most trash films fall short, this film excels and prospers. Case in point: the opening credits of the film. It shows the iconic yellow-lettering film title, as the camera tracks and follows our lead character and resident hobo Fred as he steals a bottle of liquor from an unsuspecting store owner. Fred escapes into a burning apartment building (which gives viewers the first scenes of full-frontal nudity and some grand bush!)—this sequence of shots displays professional camerawork that is relevant—no matter what film it is. There is a reason Muro went on to operate the camera for some of Hollywood's biggest and greatest Hollywood blockbusters.

Having barely tapped the surface of the comedic quirks to the characters, I must mention two of my very favorite actors in the film. First, the late and great R.L. Ryan (credited as Pat Ryan) portraying Frank Schnizer. Interacting with Arakawa, Ryan's on-the-spot ad-libbed dialogue was right on. Ryan's overweight, sexist, and sexually-frustrated character continually plays grab-ass with cute and sexy Asian secretary Wendy (played by Jane Arakawa, presently wife of Rolling Stones's back-up singer Bernard Fowler). Falling for Fred's younger brother Kevin (Mark Sferraza), she appears to make her boss jealous *and* full of wonder at the same time. Ryan is a wonderful character actor, most notable for his role as corrupt Mayor Peter Belgoody in Troma's *The Toxic Avenger* and Mr. Finley in another Troma film, *Class of Nuke 'Em High*. He even played a small role as a neighbor in the 1982 revenge flick *Fighting Back*, his first credited role on IMDB.

Ryan shows his acting chops while interacting with Arakawa during several scenes in the junkyard's office, and these are some of the funnier scenes in the entire film. In one scene, Frank is arguing with Wendy for hanging out with Kevin while bragging about his son's jobs—one working in computers and the other working as a custodial engineer at the IBM building, which one employee points out is just a glorified title for a janitor. The scenes in which Ryan and Arakawa act opposite of each other are some of the finest scenes within the film and very natural and organic.

Another actor whose performance I really enjoyed for his delivery and elements of comedy was James Lorinz, whose sarcastic delivery and classic one-liners are some of the most memorable within the whole film. His role as the loser doorman of the mob-owned Italian restaurant delivering smart-ass line after smart-ass line of total shit-talking is trash film gold! Most known for his role as Jeffrey Franken in *Frankenhooker* (another trash film worthy of repeat viewings), Mr. Lorinz seemed to be delivering punchline after punchline in machine gun-like fashion in every scene (as few as there were) that he was in.

The final aspect of a truly incredible trash film is blood and gore, which *Street Trash* has plenty of! Whether it is the incredible scenes of victims melting after drinking the 60-year-old bottles of Tenafly Viper or the epic finale in which one character loses his head (literally)—the blood and gore expectation is fulfilled. As well as containing a hearty dose of boobs and bush, *Street Trash* is my favorite trash film of all time. No other movie equals the amount of filth, sex (I mean rape), raunchy humor, nudity, colorful gore, and little-known talents all wrapped up in one big pile of entertaining garbage. I have watched *Street Trash* more than any other film in my collection, and there is a reason why. *Street Trash* does not fail to entertain and vilify the filth factor. It is the true definition of trashy entertainment. There is no higher recommendation for any film that can come higher for me than Jim Muro and Roy Frumkes's *Street Trash*.

Target Earth (1954)
by Tony Schaab

Ever heard someone spout the old tried-and-true phrase "they just don't make 'em like they used to?" Well, in the film industry that phrase is definitely true, although the resulting shift in cinematic techniques nowadays as opposed to the days gone by is both a blessing and a curse.

I have a special place in my heart for the old sci-fi B-movies of the 1950s and 1960s. Granted, I didn't grow up watching them when they were new and first released, but I have spent many a late night in front of the TV since, catching up on this intriguing sub-genre of films through my ever-growing movie collection or stumbling upon one via the magic of basic cable. And now, with Netflix and other on-demand movie services? There are literally hundreds of these golden oldies at my fingertips.

But it's a mixed bag: for every film like *Forbidden Planet* or *Night of the Living Dead* that featured a truly compelling idea whose story has stood the test of time, there are a dozen movies like *Manos: The Hands of Fate* or *Plan 9 From Outer Space* whose creators were so blinded by their intent to create something "fantastical" they slap-dashed ideas and objects together so haphazardly that the film is barely watchable for actual entertainment value.

Target Earth falls somewhere in between the two extremes. It was produced and released in 1954, on the overall forefront of the massive influx of B-movies during the time period. Its story follows a few random strangers who have seemingly missed a massive overnight evacuation of a large city (many reviews list the city in question as Chicago, but I never heard anyone in the film specifically reference where they were). After a very eerie-feeling first half of the film, where both the characters and the audience are unaware of what is truly going on, the aforementioned "fantastical" element arrives: the city has been invaded by an army of giant mechanical men from Venus who have come to slowly (very...slowly...) take over the Earth.

Can these few people trapped inside the city survive? Will the character with a shady past pose an even bigger threat than the rampaging automatons? Can the army scientists come up with a so-simple-I-can't-believe-they-didn't-think-of-it-sooner way to defeat the otherworldly invaders? Is the suspense killing you yet? No? Well...that's good, I suppose.

So, there a few big questions that any respectable movie-watcher will want answered. The first question is likely, "is the film entertaining?" Well...yes and no. As mentioned previously, the film does establish a great atmospheric vibe early on and maintains this Hitchcockian flavor for about half of the story. Sadly, though, once the threat "from beyond the stars" is revealed, things quickly spiral into just another attempt by filmmakers of the time trying to present the viewer with something they've never seen before and possibly (hopefully) won't understand. I do enjoy the first half of the film very much, but with a run time of only an hour and fifteen minutes, it's hard to think of *Target Earth* as feature-length by today's standards.

Is the film grounded in reality at all? The more astonishing elements of the film turn out to be rather blasé—giant robots! Oh wait, they're only about six feet tall...Amazingly-advanced military compounds! Oh wait, they're just in someone's basement...Shiny metallic invaders from beyond! Oh wait, they just look like upside-down washer and dryers. Some of this is forgivable—or at least understandable—due to the budgetary constraints of the time. On the flip side, the film does score highly in its characterization of the human cast of the select few left behind in the city. These people are shown with real-world problems in addition to the whole pesky robot-invasion thing—and extra points for the film opening with the surprisingly-heavy content of the aftermath of Nora's (Kathleen Crowley) failed suicide attempt.

What about the narrative itself? While the main conceit of the story could hide behind the shroud of mystery at first, once the true nature of the threat was revealed, the story just didn't have anywhere to go. Almost all of the film is spent showing how unstoppable these iron-clad monsters are...until the military scientists miraculously discover the too-simple solution at the last moment. It's kitschy, and while some kitsch can be fun kitsch, in this case it's just kitsch for kitsch's sake, and that's not the good kind of kitsch. I think I've just set the world record for number of times using the word "kitsch" in one sentence!

A big question for me is always: is the film visually presented well? Again, I understand that the film budgets of yesteryear are chump change compared to today's blockbusters (even compared to many of today's independent productions), but if *Target Earth* had any kind of budget, it was money poorly spent. In addition to looking largely ridiculous, the robot army didn't even fit that definition: the effects team only created *one* robot suit, so the viewer never sees more than a single robot in any given shot. When one of the automatons fires its death ray and vaporizes a human, the effect is eye-rollingly bad at best, and you can actually see the film jump from where the person was standing one moment and gone the next. But hey—at least the robots weren't the bodies of gorillas with deep-sea divers helmets for their heads, am I right?

In re-reading this article, I think I sound particularly harsh on this film, and that really wasn't my intent. The acting is well above-average for its time, and as I've said previously, the first half of the movie is incredibly effective as an unknown/suspense horror type of tale. Ultimately, the story has nowhere to go and falls very flat before finally copping out to an easy conclusion. If you are searching for a solid B-movie to pop in as you settle in on the couch in a dark room with a bowl of popcorn, *Target Earth* is passable, but there are far better options for you out there.

Tremors (1990)
by Catherine Chisnall

I really admire people who can craft a great movie on a small budget and *Tremors* (1990) is one of my favorites, directed by Ron Underwood and written by S.S. Wilson, Brent Maddock and Underwood. Get two well-known actors (in this case Kevin Bacon and Fred Ward), some decent lesser-known ones and don't overdo the special effects, and this movie is a satisfying and complete entertainment package. I know I am not the only fan to think so.

Despite having to watch *Tremors* on a tiny black-and-white portable television, the first thing that attracted me was the presence of Kevin Bacon, my first teenage crush and hero. Seeing him in *Footloose* was the high point of my early adolescence and I will watch any film that he stars in, unless it's really gruesome horror. *Tremors*, however, is not, and after being curious enough to watch it, I was pleased to discover the movie's other attractions.

Firstly, there are the characters. Apart from Val McKee (Kevin Bacon), a drifting workman who turns into a hero when fighting the hungry, aggressive worm-monsters which suddenly appear around the town he is working in, there is his older, dependable colleague Earl (Fred Ward) who is trying to get the rootless Val to find a nice girl, settle down and start a decent life. He is the perfect foil for Val, unimpressed by his girl chasing and youthful lack of commitment. And when the female character arrives, to my amusement she is not the blonde, large breasted giggler that Val fantasized about. She is Rhonda, a serious, intelligent scientist, who is the first to notice that things aren't right in the desert via her seismographs' unusual readings.

The survivalist couple, Burt and Heather, are essentially stereo-types—gun toting, Commie hating, American gal and guy—but their characters are fleshed out by their spoken thoughts about the monsters, their frustrations that however strong and well prepared they have been, this situation has taken them by surprise, their frustrated rivalry with Val. But in the end, human intelligence wins the day, not mechanical brute force, an interesting point made by this American film.

None of the minor characters are brought to life enough for us to care much when they get eaten by the monsters, because this is not a full-blown horror movie, and the children involved live happily ever after—phew!

And the monsters! I appreciated the fact that these "graboids" as they are dubbed by the humans, are totally unsympathetic. Not once did I feel sorry for the huge worms, or see any ounce of likeability. In so many monster movies, the "monster" is in fact a misunderstood, abused creature, such as Frankenstein, King Kong and some werewolves, such as in *An American Werewolf in London* and *The Wolfman* (the Benicio del Toro version). The graboids are Pure Evil—aggressive, ravening, slimy, indiscriminate—which makes *Tremors* a nice, simple piece of escapism from the complications of normal life where nothing is black and white.

The setting is absolutely perfect for a monster movie—the humans are completely trapped in their tiny town. The road is blocked, the phone is broken—no mobile phones in those days—and the flimsy wood buildings and worn out old vehicles are no match for the worms coming up from the ground. If any of these variables changed— another road to escape from the town by, a working phone to call for help, sturdy buildings and vehicles—the story would not work. Too many monster movies do not trap the characters believably, but *Tremors* does so expertly.

The plot is a classic monster movie structure. Luring you in slowly with the initial two bumbling characters, Val, who you just want to slap, and Earl, who you sympathize with for putting up with Val. They hear of Rhonda's unusual seismograph readings, then the creeping camera chases the unaware scientist across the ground. The duo come across a man sitting up a pylon, dead of dehydration, then sheep are found eaten, and an unknown type of snake attaches itself to Val and Earl's truck axle. Val and Earl are new in town, but something's not right around here. As they are finding things out, the audience is taken along with them, a typical plot device which works very well in this movie.

Some fun rules of monster movies can be seen in *Tremors*, such as the annoying kid who keeps crying wolf and pretending he's being attacked. Finally, when he is really attacked, the other characters ignore him—but as this film is rated PG-13, don't worry, he survives, as does the other child. The slow reveal of the monsters is a characteristic device to build tension, although in *Tremors* the creatures are revealed more quickly than in the movies of the 1950s. CGI was a very young science back in 1990, and the graboids are old fashioned practically made creatures: they are used very convincingly, because we rarely see one in its entirety, just scary parts of it, such as the snake mouths which grab their victims.

I also noticed some refreshing breaks with convention, such as when Rhonda is attacked by the worms, Val tends to her wounds after he saves her. Normally, the hero is the one to be injured and the female character cares for him afterwards. Above all, *Tremors* leaves me with a satisfied glow at the end. Brain instead of brawn defeats the monsters, good triumphs over evil, and best of all, the intelligent and thoughtful scientist, me—er—I mean Rhonda—gets her man, Kevin—I mean Val—with a passionate snog at the end. Aww...

Zombie Honeymoon (2004)
by Tony Schaab

Zombie Honeymoon is an independent, ultra-low-budget film that tries its hardest to be charming; even though it does have an interesting conceit, the film presented to the viewer is boring and wholly unrealistic, and ultimately falls flat on its face.

Director/writer/producer David Gebroe isn't totally to blame, as the inspiration for the film's story is a touching tale that's clearly very personal for him. He based the story off of true events that happened with his sister and her husband—obviously not the zombie portions, but his sister's husband was killed in a similar fashion to how the main character in *Zombie Honeymoon* dies, and this sets up the "what-if" scenario that comes with the character's reanimation.

The movie follows newlyweds Denise and Danny as they arrive for a low-key honeymoon at the Jersey shore. Their time together is interrupted, however, when a lone zombie staggers out of the water, belches black goopy stuff on Danny, and then apparently dies for real. Danny slowly turns into a zombie, and the rest of the film is spent exploring the consequences of the groom's new situation. Unfortunately, it seems that Gebroe and company—pardon the pun here—bit off a bit more than they could chew while making this movie, and the story as filmed could have used heavy edits and better acting to keep viewers' eyes from rolling in the face of total non-believability (even for a zombie film).

Zombie Honeymoon is littered from start to finish with situations that don't make sense and half-thought-out ideas that never come to fruition. I took three pages worth of notes during my second viewing of the film, and 80% of what I wrote down had directly to do with realism problems, continuity errors, and the like. Now, let me state once again that I know I'm reviewing a movie with zombies in it, and some suspension of disbelief is obviously required. This, however, does not give the creative team carte blanche to throw all aspects of reality out the window.

The knocks against the story's believable nature range from mundane (why do the doctors in the hospital act and sound like this is their first day on planet Earth? Why all the not-so-subtle references to death and reanimation both before and after Danny zombifies?) to fairly important (where did the original zombie go? Why doesn't Denise get the infection when she kisses and has sex with Zombie Danny? Why do none of Danny's victims reanimate?). These are but a small sampling of not only the problems with the film, but problems that could have been resolved with tighter writing, better editing, and more attention to the overall storyline in general.

I can certainly appreciate the plight of the independent filmmaker, having acted myself many times in local live-theater productions and friends' pet project movies alike. *Zombie Honeymoon* was picked up by Showtime and shown on their premium-cable channel before being released to DVD and, as a result of the increased visibility, this movie picks up a higher level of scrutiny than the average indie-film does.

As I tend to do when reviewing movies, I ask myself a few important questions that help me gauge how truly impactful my film-viewing experience was. The first question that always comes to my mind is "did the film entertain me?" I'm sorry to say that *Zombie Honeymoon* quickly becomes boring, and the viewer has to sit through lots of shots and scenes that can only be described as filler. Sequences like the three-minute shot of nothing but Denise driving to the store in her car simply don't need to be shown; nobody wants to watch a police officer slowly drink his soda as he spends minutes doing nothing but flipping through a scrapbook while Denise awkwardly stands by. It unequivocally feels like Gebroe was simply trying to fill time to get his story to feature-length duration. With about twenty-five minutes left to go in my first-ever viewing of the film, my DVD hiccupped and paused momentarily, and I'm sad to admit that, for a brief moment, I actually hoped the disc would totally seize up and I could have an excuse to stop watching the film. In the final fifteen minutes, the movie went from annoying me to downright pissing me off, culminating in the ridiculous and nonsensical ending. I think this story could have worked well as a 22-minute episode of a show like *The Twilight Zone* or *The Outer Limits*, but as a movie, it's just not an enjoyable experience at all.

What about the narrative itself—are there any unique points or original content of note in the movie? Of all the notes I took during my viewings, not a single one came even remotely close to noting anything positive in this area. When the existence of your zombies doesn't make sense and the rules governing your walking dead seem haphazard at best, how can you hope to be original? I'll give a lone point for the unique premise of the tale, even if the creative team totally couldn't deliver an effective presentation of it, but that's about all the positives I can give on this front.

How well is the film grounded in reality? Nada. Zero. Zip. The actors who play Danny and Denise have moments where their interactions are mildly believable, but they are few and far between. Aside from the one that infects him, Danny is the only zombie in the entire film. When you have your zombie go from relatively fine to killing and eating strangers twenty minutes later, it's not believable. When you have your zombie walk all the way down a crowded boardwalk and only attack one person in his "frenzy," it's not believable. When you have your zombie's best friend not aware of his undead condition yet "ironically" talk about what would happen if the zombie were to actually become a zombie, it's not believable. *Zombie Honeymoon*. Is. Not. Believable.

Is the film visually presented well? Sometimes a bad movie can be okay to watch if the effects are good enough to entertain, right? Sorry to say that you won't find what you're looking for here. In the early parts of the film, the viewer is asked to believe that some light skin peeling is supposed to pass for necrosis, and Danny spends most of the film *not* decomposing. Also, a healthy heaping of red paint trying to pass for blood around Danny's mouth, neck, and forehead (?) does not a convincing zombie make. When our revenant finally does start to look gruesome towards the end of the film, the makeup he's given still doesn't look good—his face and hands are so blue, it looks like he's freezing, not reanimating. And enough with the off-camera "zombie eating flesh" sound effects already! They are *not* believable and, quite frankly, a very cheap cop-out to not have to show zombie-munching carnage.

I don't mean to be overly harsh on this film, but when it's all said and done, the viewer is totally shafted on the intrinsic promise of getting eighty plus minutes of story with at least some redeeming qualities. Think of it this way: you agreed to buy a car from a man, even a used car that was coming to you in less-than-stellar condition, and instead of giving you the car, the man delivered a bicycle; it's not what you were promised, and you'd be pretty pissed, right? That metaphor, dear reader, nicely sums up the feeling I experienced when watching *Zombie Honeymoon*.

Zombiegeddon (2003)
by Andrew J. Rausch

Most of the time when you hear about this movie, it's because someone is saying that it's crap. As a producer (and actor) on this film, I could sit here and tell you it's not crap. But it kind of is. But it's that loveable kind of crap where you find yourself dismissing most of the elements that don't work and embracing those which do (or, in some cases, hilariously do not). My agreeing that this movie is crap is in no way meant as any form of disrespect. I love this goddamn movie, and I would have loved it just as much had I not been involved with it.

So what's the biggest problem with the film? It's a film flawed by design in that it served as hands-on-training/trial-by-fire for a director, producers, and crew who had absolutely no film school. This was our film school, so obviously mistakes are going to happen.

And while Chris Watson had yet to achieve the directorial glory he later would with something as accomplished as the romantic comedy *Dead in Love*, he more than makes up for any directorial deficiencies here by being one of the greatest goddamn producers I've ever had the pleasure of encountering. When it comes to production, Chris Watson is a certified genius. Hands down. No arguments.

At a time when some micro-films were starting to employ one or two known actors in them, Watson got the brilliant idea of putting together an entire ensemble of accomplished actors. Fully aware of his budget, he wisely cast two fairly-unknown actors as the leads (Ari Bavel and Paul Darrigo) and then surrounded them with a *Who's Who* of well-known actors. This cast includes—and keep in mind that this is a $10,000 picture—Julie Strain, Ron Jeremy, Joe Estevez, Robert Z'Dar, William Smith, Linnea Quigley, Brinke

Stevens, Conrad Brooks, Joe Fleishaker, Lloyd Kaufman, Trent Haaga, Tina Krause, Felissa Rose, Edwin Neal, and Tom Savini. It also features cameos by horror helmers J.R. Bookwalter and Jeff Burr.

The funny thing is, this crazy talented cast almost contained a few other notable names. I spent days on the phone with the likes of Duane Whitaker (*Pulp Fiction*), Brian O'Halloran (*Clerks*), and Mark Borchardt (*American Movie*), trying to convince them to play Jesus Christ in the movie. Borchardt was geeked out by the cast and said he'd appear in the film, then we never heard from him again. Brian O'Halloran wanted very badly to play Jesus in the film but could not because the Screen Actors Guild wouldn't let him. Interesting voice cameos that didn't make the movie were filmmakers Roger Avary, Scott Spiegel, and mega-movie-geek Harry Knowles.

So what else makes Chris Watson such a damned fine producer? Well, he managed to finagle things that wouldn't normally be seen in a micro-film, such as live tigers (we refer to them as "zombie-eating tigers"), a real-life police car (even if it was an anachronistic Barney Fife squad car), and real machine guns and squibs. The guy thought of everything. He convinced a slew of people to let us film inside their homes, and perhaps the most ingenious thing he did was to teach filmmaking at a local college in exchange for unlimited shooting access to the school's campus. I can't even begin to tell you how much money that saved us in locations.

But the truth of the matter is, *Zombiegeddon* is just plain fun. Its inherent fun has nothing to do with production values and direction (good or bad) so much as it just features the perfect ingredients for a crazy, fucked-up good time. The two leads, Bavel and Darrigo, immediately seem out of place, and yet, in some crazy way, they are exactly perfect in their roles as a couple of bad cops forced to fight off a zombie invasion. Bavel looks tough at first glance, but he's a little paunchy and comes off as a little goofy. Darrigo plays his role as a tiny, hyperactive puppy begging for attention. And yet somehow, again, they are *perfect* for their roles. Maybe it's because they seem like real people rather than over-the-top badasses like *The Shield*'s Vic Mackey or Keitel in *Bad Lieutenant*. Neither of them are particularly great thespians, but each carried with him a genuine swagger and bravado that somehow carries over onscreen. Whatever they lacked in talent, they made up for in confidence.

Watching these two goofs drive around in their squad car (which clearly reads DARE on the side) and smoke pot and talk shit is a high point of this film. The two guys are, again, inexplicably good. Most of the time screenwriter Watson fills their mouths with great dialogue, but even when the dialogue falters these two moron cops adequately keep the movie going.

The film's greatest scene, however, features Ed Neal (the hitch-hiker in the original *Texas Chainsaw Massacre*) as God. Here Neal delivers Watson's monologue as eloquently as if it were from a Eugene O'Neill play. It's just stunning to watch. As I held the boom mic for this scene, I remember someone in the crew remarking, "What the fuck? This guy is a *real* actor." Of course most of the cast was comprised of talented actors, but the point was that this guy came to play. He had his game face on and he delivered in spades.

Other highlights include Tom Savini as Jesus having a post-coital conversation with a topless Brinke Stevens (in which he says he can turn the faucet water into wine and they can party more). The zombie-eating tigers are a delight. No, they don't really look like they're eating zombies, but just seeing them in the film is a pleasure. These kinds of things just don't appear in micro-films. *Maniac Cop's* Robert Z'Dar is terrific when he chews through the scenery like a Tyrannosaurus Rex while scolding a slightly retarded-looking Ari Bavel. (Why he chose to make the goofy expression he makes in that scene is beyond me. He looks like he has to take a shit.)

This movie is just about as much fun as you can have watching a movie, at least in my estimation. It's better than the normal Troma fare and shot on about a tenth of the budget. I love, love, love this movie unapologetically, and I think Chris Watson is some sort of sick genius.

Viva la *Zombiegeddon*!

Printed in Great Britain
by Amazon